THE BEST WINES IN THE SUPERMARKETS 2024

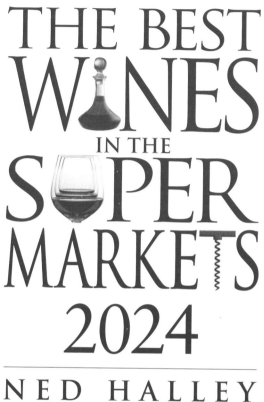

NED HALLEY

T0347206

foulsham

LONDON • NEW YORK • TORONTO • SYDNEY

W. Foulsham & Co. Ltd

for Foulsham Publishing Ltd

The Old Barrel Store, Drayman's Lane, Marlow, Bucks SL7 2FF

Foulsham books can be found in all good bookshops and direct from www.foulsham.com

ISBN: 978-0-572-04838-9

Printed and bound in Great Britain by Martins the Printers Ltd

Contents

An affordable pleasure

Welcome to the 20th successive annual edition of *The Best Wines in the Supermarkets*. Along the way, the series has reviewed about 10,000 different wines, and liked just about all of them.

From the start it's been all about affordable wines. While wine literature tends to focus on the greatest producers from classic regions such as Bordeaux and Burgundy, maybe taking in the prestige vineyards of more-distant corners of the fine-wine world, my itinerary extends little further than the nearest Co-op or Tesco.

This book's premise is that wine has become an everyday item on shopping lists. For all but a very few lovers of wine, it has to be affordable in just the way any other groceries have to be. But the range of wines on sale, especially in supermarkets, can be enormous. How to choose?

Some will answer: find a wine you like and stick to it. But look at it this way. There are up to 200,000 distinct wines on sale in the UK – we are the world's most prolific and sophisticated importer – so you could spend a lifetime relishing the task of seeking out the ones you like best.

And the ones you can afford. It is axiomatic in the wine trade that any fool can buy a great bottle of wine if money's no object. Finding one on a fixed budget is another matter altogether. In that sense, supermarket wine buyers, who must always buy to a price, are in the same boat as supermarket wine customers. Talking to wine professionals over the years, I am convinced they understand very well what it is to love wine, and what a wonderful thing it is to find something genuinely delicious that is affordable. To get such wines to market is a worthwhile vocation.

Naturally, I think wine is important. Dare I say I wouldn't like to be without it. I am well aware that the demon drink can do harm, but on balance I'm confident there is a case for the occasional adult beverage.

And so to the 2024 edition of this guide. This year, the emphasis is more than ever on affordability. The squeeze on household incomes, the rather frightening persistence of inflation and new, punitive excise duty rates on alcohol introduced in 2023 conspire to make wine prices uncomfortably topical.

The supermarkets, suspected in some circles of profiteering in the present climate, have shown remarkable restraint in putting up wine prices. I suspect the new duty level, which adds 44p to the cost of a typical bottle, will soon force up prices of cheaper wines, but I believe the retailers will continue to minimise the damage through promotional discounting.

Deals on wine in supermarkets are now institutional. All ten of the retailers featured in this book make price reductions on some or all of their ranges a perpetual if not a permanent feature. Even the two burgeoning 'discounters' Aldi and Lidl now further cut the cost of selected wines on a regular basis.

At the wine tastings generously laid on by these companies for scribblers like me, I have been asking the wine teams why they do it. It's an impertinent question, I suppose, so I should not be surprised by the evasiveness of the answers I get. The gist of it is that any retailer who steps out of line in this respect will probably soon be stepping out of business. Customers who buy wine in supermarkets expect discounts, and if there aren't any, they'll shop elsewhere.

As customers, we should incentivise the retailers into continuing with this admirable policy. We should take a very deliberate approach. Wait for the next 25%-off blanket offer and buy in bulk. It's simple enough to keep up with forthcoming promos across the market by looking online. And remember, if you are buying a case or two at a time, orders of sufficient value often qualify for free home delivery.

Duty bound

The new alcohol excise duty regime mooted by then Chancellor Rishi Sunak in his autumn Budget of 2021 finally came into force in August 2023. For wine consumers, the major change is that the rate of duty is now linked to the alcohol content of the wine. The old oddity of taxing sparkling wine higher than still wine has been excised, so to speak. So, the duty on champagne at 12.5% alcohol is now the same on a bottle of claret at 12.5% alcohol.

The new figures look like this: excise per 75cl sparkling wine (12%) falls from £2.86 to £2.67; on still wine (12.5%) rises from £2.23 to £2.67; on fortified wine such as fino sherry, at 15% from £2.23 to £3.21; fortified wine such as port at 20% from £2.98 to £4.28.

One concession. Wine between 11.5% and 14.5% alcohol will be treated as if it is 12.5% for the purposes of calculating the charge to alcohol duty until 1 February 2025.

So that's all good then. But there's another thing. The government is returning to the index-linking of duty rates after what has been quite a long pause. This is the statement: "Alcohol duty rates have remained frozen since Autumn Budget 2020. On 19 December 2022, the government extended the current alcohol duty freeze by six months from 1 February to 1 August 2023 to provide certainty to businesses. Although the public finances assume a Retail Price Index increase each February, in practice the government has enacted numerous cuts or freezes to alcohol duties over the past decade."

Thank you very much, I suppose we should all chorus. But there's bad news: on the date in February 2023 when the new rate was fixed, the RPI stood at 10.1%. That adds 44p to the price of a typical bottle of wine.

If inflation continues at present alarming levels, there could be trouble ahead. In the meantime, stock up and enjoy.

It's all about the grape variety

The grape, naturally, counts for everything in wine. The finished product is, after all, simply the fermented juice of the fruit. Well, yes, there will be a cultured yeast introduced to assist the process. And there are permitted additives, mostly sulphur products and clarifying agents, to ensure healthy, bright wine. The wine's natural sugars and acids can be supplemented.

But the grape variety still sets the pace. Dark-skinned grapes make red wine because the skins are included in the must (pressed juice) during fermentation and give the wine its colour. The juice of virtually all grapes is clear. You can make white wine with dark-skinned grapes by extracting the juice promptly and fermenting it free of the skins. The base wine for Champagne is made largely from dark-skinned grapes. But still white wine is made much more simply – from pale-skinned grapes fermented without their skins.

Different grape varieties produce correspondingly different wines. There are hundreds of distinct varieties, but a couple of dozen account for most production. All of us have favourites, or at least preferences. The varieties described here account for most of the wines on offer in the supermarkets.

Red wine varieties

Aglianico: Ancient variety of southern Italy said to have been imported by immigrant Greek farmers around 500 BC. The name is a recent rendering of former Ellenico ('Hellenic') and the grape has caught on again thanks to Aglianico del Vulture, a volcanic DOC of Basilicata. The wines are dark, intense, pungent and long-lived.

Barbera: The most widely planted dark-skinned grape of Piedmont in northwest Italy makes easy-drinking purple vigorous rasping red wine to enjoy young and also, increasingly, a darker, denser but still vigorous style given gravitas through oak-ageing. Mostly sold under denominations Barbera d'Asti and Barbera d'Alba. Unrelated to Barbaresco, a Piedmontese wine made from Nebbiolo grapes.

Cabernet Sauvignon: Originally of Bordeaux and the mainstay of claret, Cabernet berries are compact and thick-skinned, making wine of intense flavour and gripping tannin. The grandest wines need decades to develop their full bloom. Everyday wines made worldwide typically have dense colour, purple in youth, aromas of blackcurrants and cedar wood ('cigar box') and firm, juicy-savoury fruit.

Gamay: It's the grape of Beaujolais. Colour can be purple with a blue note; nose evokes new-squashed raspberries with perhaps a pear drop or two, the effect of carbonic maceration, the Beaujolais method of vinification. Fruit flavours are juicy, bouncing, even refreshing.

Grenache: The French name for the Garnacha, originally of Spain, where it is much employed in Rioja and other classic regions. HQ in France is the southern Rhône Valley with further widespread plantings across the country's Mediterranean regions. Wines can be light in colour but emphatic in flavour with a wild, hedgerow-fruit style lifted with spice and pepper. Widely cultivated across the New World.

Malbec: The signature grape of Argentina. A native of Bordeaux, where it plays a minor blending role, it thrives in the high-altitude vineyards of Mendoza, a province of the Andean foothills. The best wines have dark colour and a perfume sometimes fancifully said to evoke leather and liquorice; flavours embrace briary black fruits with suggestions of bitter chocolate, plum and spice.

Merlot: Bordeaux variety very often partnering Cabernet Sauvignon in claret blends and also solo in fabled Pomerol wines including Château Petrus. The grape is large and thin-skinned compared to Cabernet, making wine of rich ruby colour with scents evoking black cherry and cassis and fruit that can be round and rich. Ordinary wines are soft, mellow and early developing but might lack the firmness of tannin that gives balance.

Pinot Noir: It's the solo grape of proper red burgundy and one of three varieties in champagne. Everyday Pinot wines typically have a bright, translucent ruby colour and aromas evoking red soft summer fruits and cherries. Flavours correspond. Fine Pinot has elegant weight and shape, mysteriously alluring. New Zealand makes distinctive, delicious, sinewy Pinots; Chile produces robust and earthy Pinots; California's best Pinots compare for quality with fabulously expensive Burgundies.

Sangiovese: The grape of Chianti, so-named after the Latin for 'the blood of Jove', makes pleasingly weighted, attractively coloured wines with plummy perfume, even pruny in older wines, and slinky flavours evoking blackcurrant, raspberry and occasionally nectarine. Good Chianti always has a clear tannic edge, giving the wine its trademark nutskin-dry finish.

Syrah: At home in southern France, the Syrah makes wines that at their best are densely coloured, rich in aromas of sun-baked blackberries, silky in texture and plumply, darkly, spicily flavoured. The grandest pure-Syrah wines, such as Hermitage and Côte Rôtie, are gamey, ripe and rich and very long-lived. Syrah is widely planted across Mediterranean France as a blending grape in wines of the Côtes du Rhône and Languedoc. Under the name Shiraz, Syrah is Australia's most prolific red-wine variety.

Tempranillo: The grape at the heart of Rioja has to work hard. The unique selling point of the region's famous red wines is the long ageing process in oak casks that gives the finished product its creamy, vanilla richness – which can all too easily overwhelm the juiciness and freshness of the wine. The Tempranillo's bold blackcurranty-minty aromas and flavours stand up well to the test, and the grape's thick skin imparts handsome ruby colour that doesn't fade as well as firm tannins that keep the wine in shape even after many years in cask or bottle. Tempranillo is widely planted throughout Spain, and in Portugal, under numerous assumed names.

White wine varieties

Albariño: Rightly revered Iberian variety once better known in its Minho Valley, Portugal, manifestation as Alvarinho, a mainstay of vinho verde wine. Since the 1980s, Albariño from Spain's Galicia region, immediately north of Portugal, has been making aromatic and scintillatingly racy sea-fresh dry white wines from vineyards often planted close to the Atlantic shore. The seaside DO of Rias Baixas, now a major centre for gastro-tourism, is the heart of Albariño country. The variety, characterized by small, thick-skinned berries with many pips, is now also cultivated in California, New Zealand and beyond.

Chardonnay: Universal variety still at its best at home in Burgundy for simple appley fresh dry wines all the way up to lavish new-oak-fermented deluxe appellations such as Meursault and Montrachet making ripe, complex, creamy-nutty and long-developing styles. Imitated in Australia and elsewhere with mixed success.

Chenin Blanc: Loire Valley variety cultivated for dry, sweet and sparkling white wines, some of them among France's finest. Honeyed aromas and zesty acidity equally characterize wines including elegant, mineral AOP Vouvray and opulent, golden late-harvested AOP Coteaux du Layon. In South Africa, Chenin Blanc now makes many fascinating and affordable wines.

Fiano: Revived southern Italian variety makes dry but nuanced wines of good colour with aromas of orchard fruit, almonds and candied apricots and finely balanced fresh flavours. Fleetingly fashionable and worth seeking out.

Glera: Widely planted in the Veneto region of northeast Italy, it's the principal variety in prosecco sparkling wine. The grape itself used to be named prosecco, after the winemaking village of Prosecco near Treviso, but under a 2009 change to the wine-denomination rules, the name can now be applied exclusively to the wine, not the grape. Glera makes a neutral base wine with plenty of acidity. It is a prolific variety, and needs to be. Sales of prosecco in Britain have now surpassed those of champagne.

Palomino Fino: The grape that makes sherry. The vines prosper in the *albariza*, the sandy, sun-bleached soil of Andalucia's Jerez region, providing a pale, bone-dry base wine ideally suited to the sherry process. All proper sherry of every hue is white wine from Palomino Fino. The region's other grape, the Pedro Ximenez, is used as a sweetening agent and to make esoteric sweet wines.

Pinot Grigio: At home in northeast Italy, it makes dry white wines of pale colour and frequently pale flavour too. The mass-market wines' popularity might owe much to their natural low acidity. The better wines are aromatic, fleetingly smoky and satisfyingly weighty in the manner of Pinot Gris made in the French province of Alsace. New Zealand Pinot Gris or Pinot Grigio follows the Alsace style.

Riesling: Native to Germany, it makes unique wines pale in colour with sharp-apple aromas and racy, sleek fruit whether dry or sweet according to labyrinthine local winemaking protocols. Top-quality Rhine and Mosel Rieslings age wonderfully, taking on golden hues and a fascinating 'petrolly' resonance. Antipodean Rieslings have more colour and weight often with a mineral, limey twang.

Sauvignon Blanc: Currently fashionable thanks to New Zealand's inspired adoption of the variety for assertive, peapod-nettle-seagrass styles. Indigenous Sauvignons from France's Loire Valley have rapidly caught up, making searingly fresh wines at all levels from generic Touraine up to high-fallutin' Sancerre. Delicate, elegant Bordeaux Sauvignon is currently on top form too.

Semillon: Along with Sauvignon Blanc, a key component of white Bordeaux, including late-harvested, golden sweet wines such as Sauternes. Even in dry wines, colour ranges up to rich yellow, aromas evoke tropical fruits and honeysuckle, exotic flavours lifted by citrus presence. Top Australian Semillons rank among the world's best.

Viognier: Formerly fashionable but perpetually interesting variety of the Rhône Valley makes white wines of pleasing colour with typical apricot aroma and almondy-orchardy fruit; styles from quite dry to fruitily plump.

More about these varieties and many others in 'A wine vocabulary' starting on page 152.

Brand awareness

Big-brand wines such as Blossom Hill and Hardy do not crowd the pages of this book. I do get to taste them, and leave most of them out. I believe they don't measure up for quality, interest or value.

The best wines in the supermarkets are very often own-brands. Own-brands date back to the 1970s, when interest in wine finally began to take root in Britain. Sainsbury's was first, with its own Claret, about 1975. It was hardly a revolutionary idea. Grand merchants like Berry Bros & Rudd (est 1698) had been doing own-label Bordeaux and much else besides, for ever.

In the supermarket sector, wine was bought on the wholesale market like anything else, from butter to washing powder. Only when interest in wine started to extend beyond the coterie served by the merchants did the mass retailers take any notice. It was thanks, of course, to the new craze for foreign travel, and to the good influence of writers like Elizabeth David, who revealed the joys of Continental-style food and drink. In 1966, Hugh Johnson's brilliant and accessible book *Wine* piqued the public consciousness as never before.

The adoption of supermarket wine was slow enough, but accelerated in the 1980s by the arrival of new, decent wines from Australia. Earlier on, cheap Aussie wines had been overripe, stewed rubbish, but breakthrough technology now enabled fresh, bold reds and whites of a different stripe. Wretched Europlonk brands like Hirondelle retreated before a tide of lush Chardonnay and 'upfront' Shiraz.

The horizon for supermarket wine buyers, always shackled by price constraint, was suddenly widened. In spite of the delivery distances, southern hemisphere producers could match their Old World counterparts for value as well as interest and quality.

In time, the winemakers of Europe fought back. Top estates carried on with 'fine wine' production, but humbler enterprises had to learn how to master real quality at the everyday level. They did. I believe the huge improvements in the simpler wines of the Continent owe much to the need to match the competition from the New World.

By the 1990s, Britain had become the world's biggest wine importer. Supermarkets were largely responsible, and now had muscle in the market. They started to dispatch their own people to vineyards and wineries worldwide, not just to buy the wines but to participate in their production. And always, they demanded the lowest-possible prices.

And so to today's proliferation of supermarket own-brands. They are the flagships of every one of the big grocers, and usually the focal point of promotions. They are, naturally enough, the wines of which their begetters are most proud. Mass-market brands do still persist in the supermarkets. Some are very good. I think of Blason, Chasse and Vieille Ferme from France; Baron de Ley and Miguel Torres from Spain; McGuigan and Penfolds from Australia; Catena from Argentina and Concha y Toro from Chile, among others.

If you have a favourite popular brand, do check the index to this book on page 156. It might not be mentioned in the entry for the supermarket where you're used to finding it, but that doesn't mean I've left it out.

Pick of the year

Thirty-five out of the 500 wines commended this year have achieved the signal honour of a maximum 10 score. It's based on best wine at best price – very much a value judgment – but really it's just a bit of fun. Taste as we all know is highly subjective in all matters, and so is any notion of value.

But for what it's worth, the honours this time are allotted on a country-of-origin basis as follows: France first with 15. Runners-up by a distance (I didn't really see this coming) are Italy, South Africa and Spain each on 4, then Australia, England and Germany on 2 and singletons Chile and Portugal.

Retailer rankings are a bit more even. Waitrose first (obvs) with 9, Morrisons and Tesco with 5 apiece, followed by Aldi, the Co-op, Lidl and M&S each with 3, Asda on 2 and Majestic and Sainsbury's as singletons.

In one respect there really is a sign of change from previous chartings. Aldi and Lidl are suddenly both in the running. I ought to point out that these two discounters have wine ranges far less wide in number and diversity than the biggest of their rivals, so the wines I've picked out in tastings do come from a much smaller pool. If I were ranking the overall offerings of the ten retailers featured in this book, suffice it to say I wouldn't put either Aldi or Lidl above, say, Marks & Spencer.

Naturally, I look forward to the discounters continuing to compete with their more-established rivals in the way of wine. I have never really believed that the German pair have outclassed any other retailer in terms of value-for-money wines, especially with price promotions now so frequent and so generous among the big multiples.

What interests me is the continuing improvement in the quality of wines in all the supermarkets. It's happening, and it's a very good thing.

Red wines

Villa Verde Montepulciano d'Abruzzo 2022	Morrisons	£6.00
Mimo Moutinho Lisbon Red 2021	Aldi	£6.29
Specially Selected Aglianico del Vulture 2020	Aldi	£7.99
Château Vieux Manoir 2020	Co-op	£8.50
Marques de Caltrava Reserva Tempranillo 2015	Waitrose	£8.99
Mongravet 2021	Waitrose	£9.99
Terre de Fiano Organic Primitivo 2021	Waitrose	£9.99
Vergelegen Cabernet Sauvignon Merlot Fairtrade 2019	Co-op	£10.00
Triguedina Jean-Luc Baldès Malbec du Clos 2019	Waitrose	£10.99
Juliénas Les Mouilles Pardon & Fils 2021	Majestic	£11.00
d'Arenberg The Footbolt Shiraz 2021	Tesco	£12.50
Wirra Wirra Church Block Cabernet Sauvignon-Shiraz-Merlot 2020	Asda	£13.00
M&S Collection El Duque del Miralta Grand Reserva Rioja 2016	Marks & Spencer	£16.00
Finest Châteauneuf du Pape	Tesco	£21.00

White wines

Bräuneberger Kurfürstlay Riesling Mosel 2021	Lidl	£5.29
M&S This is Chardonnay 2022	Marks & Spencer	£6.20
Specially Selected South African Rhone Blend 2021	Aldi	£6.99
Dr L Riesling 2021	Asda	£7.00
Taste the Difference Jurançon Sec 2021	Sainsbury's	£8.00
Finest Soave Classico Superiore 2021	Tesco	£8.25
Finest Valle de Leyda Chardonnay 2022	Tesco	£8.50
Paul Mas Réserve Languedoc Blanc 2022	Waitrose	£9.99
Reyneke Organic Chenin Blanc 2022	Waitrose	£9.99
The Best Vouvray 2021	Morrisons	£11.00
Alsace Pinot Gris Réserve 2021	Waitrose	£11.99
Les Domaines Brocard Organic Chablis 2021 Marks & Spencer		£17.00
The Best Chablis Premier Cru 2020	Morrisons	£20.00

Fortified wines

The Best Palo Cortado Sherry	Morrisons	£6.50
Pedro's Almacenista Oloroso Sherry	Waitrose	£11.49

Sparkling wines

Crémant de Loire Brut	Lidl	£8.99
Carpentier Champagne Brut	Lidl	£13.99
Les Pionniers Champagne Brut	Co-op	£22.75
Finest Premier Cru Champagne Brut	Tesco	£25.00
The Best English Sparkling Wine 2010	Morrisons	£27.00

Aldi

The German discounter now ranks fourth among the supermarkets, lately pipping Morrisons for annual sales. That's some going: Aldi has only appeared in the pages of this book at all since the 2015 edition, when there were 300 stores in Britain. In 2023, that total went past 1,000.

In this year's guide, there are 48 Aldi wines commended. That's a good rate of qualification from a range that's still below 200 different lines. Aldi might offer a narrower choice than its mainstream rivals – all the wines are exclusive; there are no global brands – but the range has unquestionably come of age.

Julie Ashfield, the chain's UK buying boss, has this to say: *"Aldi is growing rapidly and outperforming competitors like never before, and much of this is thanks to our successful wine ranges."*

Yup, Aldi takes its wine seriously. But contrary to what might be the expectation, price is by no means the principal attraction. Tasting a hundred or so of the wines this year, I have found the really cheap bottles only so-so. It's above the £5-to-6 mark they start to score.

But there you are. In many respects Aldi competes more and more effectively in the middle market. Among this year's picks from the wines, I've top-scored two inspiring reds from Italy and Portugal and an extraordinary white from South Africa.

If I have any complaint, it's that Aldi so neglects the wines of its fatherland. The fabled rieslings of Germany are poorly represented in UK supermarkets and surely an enterprise founded in the Rhineland, as Aldi was in 1946, could do a little more to honour its roots, so to speak.

RED WINES

ARGENTINA

🍷 8 Specially Selected Argentinian Shiraz 2021 £6.79
Liked the polo pony on the label and the wine didn't disappoint. In a pleasant change from malbec, here the shiraz/syrah brings concentrated blackberry fruit and warm spice to the well-knit flavours and there's wholesome grip at the finish; 13.5% alcohol.

🍷 8 Specially Selected Argentinian Malbec 2021 £8.99
This nicely made Uco Valley (Mendoza) pure varietal honours the region's good name for characterful malbec. Good abrasion in the black fruit makes it a great meat-matcher, and there's fine balance and weight; 14% alcohol.

AUSTRALIA

🍷 8 Kooliburra Australian Shiraz Cabernet 2021 £4.69
Recognisable blend of plumply ripe shiraz with brisk blackcurrant cabernet; works well for balance and heft; 13% alcohol. Kooliburra might sound like a made-up brand but is, apparently, an actual winery.

**🍷 8 Chapter & Verse Australian
Cabernet Sauvignon 2021** £5.25
Easy-drinking, bright, freshly juicy, firm black-fruit party red; 13.5% alcohol. Liked this better than the merlot sold under the same heading. Chapter & Verse, incidentally, is a generic range by mega-winery Hardys. The brand, I like to think, commemorates English novelist and poet Thomas Hardy, whose namesake, a Devon-born farmer, founded the firm in Australia in 1853.

🍷 8 Specially Selected Pinot Noir 2022 £7.49
It's as ripe (and 14% alcohol) as you might expect for a pinot from South Australia, but this one's nicely balanced between strawberry-raspberry sweetness and poised acidity with a lick of creaminess from (I suppose) oak contact. Artful, likeable contrivance.

RED WINES

AUSTRALIA

♟ 8 **Specially Selected Clare Valley Shiraz 2021** £8.99
Immediately impressive full-blown dark and soupy Clare wine, this is the real thing at a fair price; 14% alcohol. Safe bet.

♟ 8 **Specially Selected Australian Malbec 2021** £9.79
If you'd like a diversion from Argentine malbec, try this Padthaway version: big, forward, cushiony fruit with a distinct liquorice lift makes interesting and satisfying drinking; 14.5% alcohol.

CHILE

♟ 7 **Estevez Chilean Cabernet Sauvignon 2022** £4.29
Callow-looking but with wholesome cassis-savour; ripe food wine with friendly grip; 13% alcohol. Keen price.

FRANCE

♟ 8 **Pierre Jaurant French Fitou 2021** £6.99
Really quite a hefty spin on the old Fitou theme, once a star of the Languedoc, this has dark hedgerow fruits, warm garrigue spice and a generous, saucy richness; 14% alcohol. Nice winter red for grilled meats and cassoulet.

♟ 8 **Specially Selected Cairanne 2021** £8.99
Rather opulent Côtes du Rhône village cru combining sunny ripeness of red fruits with warm spice in the authentic regional style; 14% alcohol.

♟ 9 **Specially Selected Pézenas 2020** £9.99
Pézenas is a picturesque little town of the Hérault in Mediterranean France which has lately been awarded its own wine appellation. Well done Aldi for finding this rare example: it's slinkily dark and rich featuring plummy, herby savours trimmed with savoury tannins – should age well in bottle; 14% alcohol.

RED WINES

FRANCE

♈ 8 **Château Pérenne Côtes de Bordeaux 2016** £9.99
This well-formed and developed mainly-merlot in the modern ('fruit-forward') Bordeaux style is sleek and balanced and really quite elegant; 14% alcohol. From the relatively unknown Bordeaux outpost of Blaye, it rates only the humble Côtes appellation, but it's a very proper kind of claret.

ITALY

♈ 10 **Specially Selected Aglianico del Vulture 2020** £7.99
This irresistibly named prodigy from Italy's Basilicata region is terrifically good at this price. Intense smoky-spicy blackberry-chocolate-cherry fruit, baked bordering on burnt in its ripeness and plumped by oak contact; properly nutskin-dry at the edge to make a fine partner to sticky pasta as well as meaty dishes; 14.5% alcohol. Aglianico is the vine, cultivated since ancient Roman times (imported by earlier Greek settlers), and Vulture the vast sleeping volcano on whose brimstone slopes and fringes the vineyards lie.

LEBANON

♈ 8 **Specially Selected Lebanese Red 2020** £8.99
Vin Rouge du Liban it's styled and is suitably contrived from French grape varieties cabernet sauvignon, cinsault, syrah and carignan as a pale-ish, pleasingly raspy but sweetly ripe blend in the exotic, tobacco-and-baked-fruit mould of that famed and expensive Bekaa-Valley icon Chateau Musar; 13.5% alcohol. Distinctively alluring.

PORTUGAL

♈ 10 **Mimo Moutinho Lisbon Red 2021** £6.29
Standout red from syrah blended with red-juiced Alicante bouschet (wine grapes are almost invariably white-juiced) and the great Port grape touriga nacional. It's from the loosely defined Lisboa region north of the Portuguese capital, source of interesting and undervalued wines such as this delicious item: dark and mysterious with savoury brambly-porty fruits, exotic notions of clove and cinnamon, healthy tannin and 13% alcohol. Grippingly good, versatile food matcher.

RED WINES

PORTUGAL

♈ 9 Mimo Moutinho Dão 2021 £6.79

The Dão appellation, one of Portugal's oldest, was once notorious for hard-tasting tannic reds from obscure regional grapes, but has long since branched out into more useful varieties like the touriga nacional, noblest of the Port grapes, that constitute the entirety of this deliciously slinky item. Typical spicy-clovey Portuguese style to the darkly minty fruit, easy weight, fine balance; 13% alcohol.

♈ 8 Animus Douro Red 2021 £6.49

Convincing table red from Port country with a dark minty grip echoing the fortified wine; savoury and satisfying; 13.5% alcohol.

♈ 8 Animus Douro Grande Reserva £9.99 £9.99

Sturdy Port-country table wine; darkly rich with ripened black fruits and oaky creaminess but poised and agreeably weighted; 14% alcohol. Special-occasion winter red that should age gracefully.

SOUTH AFRICA

♈ 8 Cambalala South African Shiraz 2022 £4.29

There's an agreeable weight to this warmly spicy and plummy pure varietal; 13% alcohol. One of several decent Cape bargains at Aldi this year.

♈ 8 Cambalala South African Malbec 2022 £5.99

Hearty Cape venture into Argentine territory, smartly packaged, darkly ripe and complete; 13% alcohol.

RED WINES

Y 8 **Grapevine Shiraz** £3.89

From Aldi's emphatically entry-level 'Grapevine' range I liked this one best: full, rounded, spicy and sweetly ripe blend from two regions, La Mancha and Jumilla, from more than one vintage; 12.5% alcohol. Cautionary note: the quoted price might well have lifted by now thanks to the 44p lift in excise duty from August 2023.

Y 9 **Baron Amarillo Rioja Reserva 2017** £5.99

It's the genuine article: slick, minty-creamy-cassis, recognisable, mature Rioja with bright fruit and generous weight (13.5% alcohol) at a giveaway price.

Y 8 **Specially Selected Californian Pinot Noir 2021** £7.99

Delicate in bricky colour and light in body this is nevertheless a firmly textured and integrated earthy-cherry pinot of ripeness and character; 13.5% alcohol. A pleasant surprise and a wine you might want to try cool from the fridge.

PINK WINES

Y 8 **Chassaux et Fils Atlantique Rosé 2022** £6.49

Salmon-pink cabernet sauvignon-based wine from coastal Bordeaux with pleasingly ripe blackcurrant/redcurrant fruit and a twang of citrus acidity; fresh and interesting; 12% alcohol.

Y 8 **Specially Selected Ventoux Rosé 2022** £6.99

The wholesome shell-pink colour and palpable fruit impact from this grenache-led superior Rhône rosé make for an unusually memorable glassful, notably dry and crisp with a little peppery savour; 13% alcohol.

PINK WINES

🍷 8 Specially Selected Costières de Nîmes Rosé 2021 £7.99
Reassuring smoked-salmon colour and bright redcurrant and raspberry perfume introduce this classy syrah-based Mediterrranean pink – lots of eager summer soft fruit, crisp and tangy, nicely balanced; 12.5% alcohol. Not cheap but a rosé you might well remark on.

🍷 8 Specially Selected Toscana Organic Rosé 2022 £7.49
It's from the Chianti grape, sangiovese, and you get the cherry-raspberry hallmark fruit in delicate traces through the soft but clean-finishing savour with warm spicy-herby notes; 13% alcohol.

WHITE WINES

🍷 8 Specially Selected Australian Viognier 2022 £6.49
Lively variation on the French viognier theme of plump fruit-salad flavours, this artfully balances hothouse-fruit savours with apple crispness capped by a clean nectarine acidity; 13.5% alcohol.

🍷 8 Pierre Jaurant Chardonnay 2022 £6.79
The label appears to depict Johnnie Walker of scotch whisky renown but this, I promise, is a decent Languedoc dry wine, bright and ripe with melon and peach fruit; 13.5% alcohol.

🍷 8 Specially Selected Picpoul de Pinet 2022 £7.99
It's all here: snappy saline Mediterranean refresher made for oysters and mussels from an understandably popular appellation not far from the seaside resort of Sète; 12.5% alcohol.

WHITE WINES

FRANCE

🍷 8 **Specially Selected Roussanne 2022**   £7.99
Generously coloured and ripe peachy-apricot Pays d'Oc, neatly trimmed with citrus acidity; easy to like and a nifty match for shellfish; 13% alcohol.

GERMANY

🍷 8 **Blütengarten Rheinhessen Riesling 2021**   £4.69
I expect a German enterprise to do more for its native wine industry than Aldi does (in fairness, last year's fine Ockfener Bockstein Riesling Kabinett was a nod in the right direction) but this QbA at a basic price will have to suffice this year: grapey-appley and soft, a decent fresh aperitif wine; 11% alcohol.

GREECE

🍷 8 **Athlon Assyrtiko 2022**   £7.99
Holiday dry white from Macedonia with bright orchard fruit; crisp and pleasantly raspy; 12% alcohol.

🍷 8 **Filos Alpha Estate Chardonnay 2022**   £8.99
Rather lush pure varietal in a smart package from Amyndeon in northern Greece balancing minerality and creamy oak; 13% alcohol. Makes an impression.

ITALY

🍷 7 **Grapevine Pinot Grigio**   £3.99
If it has to be PG, try this non-vintage party glugger (see that? PG!) for size. The price looks the main draw but in fairness it's a decent softly fruity blend with 10% chardonnay plus smatterings of riesling and pinot noir that delivers something of the proper PG style with a trace of smokiness, and finishes healthily crisp; 11.5% alcohol. It's from Lombardy in north-west Italy rather than from the main PG lake, the Veneto in the north-east, and maybe that helps.

WHITE WINES

ITALY

🍷 8 Castellore Organic Pinot Grigio
Delle Venezie 2021 £5.99
Sherbetty refreshment alongside gently smoky orchard fruits conspire to give this Veneto PG a novel merit: likeable character. I only tried it because it came in an unusual pot-shape bottle, and I can only commend it; 12% alcohol.

🍷 8 Castellore Sicilian Grillo 2021 £6.99
Been to Sicily? This attractively packaged dry table wine from a grape once known only in the island's sticky Marsala positively evokes the herby maquis of its baked landscapes, lit up by ripe citrus perfumes and flavours; fascinating, heady, glyceriney stuff to match assertive menus; 12.5% alcohol.

NEW ZEALAND

🍷 8 Freeman's Bay Sauvignon Blanc 2022 £6.79
Crisp, sweet green pepper style with a spike of citrus, discreetly plumped with added chardonnay – a crafty variation on the familiar Kiwi theme; 12.5% alcohol.

🍷 9 Freeman's Bay Marlborough
Sauvignon Blanc 2022 £6.99
This unadulterated companion wine to the wine immediately above is quite distinct: crunchy-crisp grassy green fruit, impressively mouthfilling and lasting; 12.5% alcohol. Good value.

PORTUGAL

🍷 7 Animus Vinho Verde 2022 £4.99
This positively fizzing example of the popular Minho Valley refresher is just short of confected – not dry but fresh as well as lively; 11% alcohol.

WHITE WINES

8 Mimo Moutinho Portuguese Avesso 2021 £5.99
Avesso is a lesser-known grape variety grown for vinho verde, here making a non-prickly version of the wine that is nevertheless keenly brisk and green with only a trace of confection; 12.5% alcohol. If you enjoy VV, it's worth a try.

8 Cambalala South African Sauvignon Blanc 2022 £4.75
Aldi is very keen on sauvignon blanc, showing no fewer than 13 different samples on the tasting day. I liked this one for value: grassy and green-pepper fresh with twangy-lemony lift; 12.5% alcohol.

8 Cambalala South African Viognier 2022 £5.99
Fresh floral aroma followed up by ripe orchard fruits with a lick of candied apricot amid the plump ripeness in the approved viognier manner, this is a nicely balanced dry wine for fishy feasts and salads; 12% alcohol.

**10 Specially Selected South African
Rhone Blend 2021** £6.99
Show-off wine that amply demonstrates the skills of the Cape's winemakers by assembling grenache blanc, roussanne and marsanne grown in the well-rated Voor-Paardeberg region to make a plush dry white, credibly comparable to the grandest vin blanc of the southern Rhône Valley, Châteauneuf du Pape. It's a lovely contrivance of aromas and flavours evoking orchard and stone fruits, cushiony with ample ripeness but brisk in its freshness and long on contemplative aftertastes; 13.5% alcohol. Must try.

WHITE WINES

8 Baron Amarillo Rueda Verdejo 2022 £5.29

Attractively coloured, zesty, dry green-fruit example of dependable Verdejo, the grape that's made the obscure Rueda region famous for Spain's answer to sauvignon blanc; a good-value introduction to a wine style well worth getting to know; 13.5% alcohol.

8 Specially Selected Monastrell Blanco 2022 £6.99

From Alicante, it's akin to Verdejo (see Rueda wine above) but made as a 'blanc de noir' from the free-run juice of black grape variety monastrell. Attractive gold colour, interesting grassy, fino-sherry aromas and nuanced orchard and preserved fruit flavours; 12% alcohol. Versatile food matcher.

FORTIFIED WINES

8 Fletchers 10-Year-Old Tawny Port £10.99

Christmas special always worth looking out for. Still ruby in colour but showing a little copper ('tawny') at the rim, heady figgy-honey aroma, quite light in body, a touch fiery and copious in Christmas-cake savours, very sweet and pleasing; 20% alcohol.

SPARKLING WINES

9 Specially Selected Crémant du Jura 2019 £8.99

A perpetual favourite sparkler from the mountain country of eastern France and pure chardonnay: seductive, ripe, sweet-apple freshness conveyed in a creamy flow of persisting tiny bubbles – distinctive and delightful; 12% alcohol.

SPAIN

PORTUGAL

FRANCE

SPARKLING WINES

8 **Veuve Monsigny Champagne Brut** £14.99

The price is moving up (it was £12.49 last time I tasted it) but the quality of Aldi's house Champagne is consistent: lively mousse delivering the easy yeasty fruit with its lemon twang and trace of mellow richness to good effect; 12.5% alcohol.

8 **Veuve Monsigny Champagne Rosé Brut** £16.99

The brazen pink colour lures you into the sunny strawberry nose and bright corresponding fruit; lively in mousse and savour, it's refreshing and somehow actually tastes pink – a winner; 12.5% alcohol.

Asda

Just five of the 35 wines I've picked out from Asda this year are priced at £6 or under. It's a sign of the times, of course, what with inflation and the leap in excise duty, but there's a clue here too to the changes I believe are taking place at Asda itself.

The Extra Special own-label brand, introduced about 15 years ago to offer quality wines at affordable prices, bloomed into a range comparable with those of any of Asda's rivals. I have consistently reported that ES wines made Asda the go-to supermarket for the best of bargains of genuine worth. But the range has started to wither. Only half the wines featured here this year are Extra Special. Many old friends have been let go.

There is, I'm happy to say, consolation to be found among bought-in brands, including legendary red Wirra Wirra Church Block from Australia, sublime rieslings from Trimbach in Alsace and Dr Loosen in the Mosel, and a fine malbec from one of Argentina's great names, Viñalba, at a keen price.

And there's further cheer in Asda's evolving policies of discounting wines. As well as the long-established 'roll-back' scheme of reducing prices on selected bottles there are now regular across-the-range multibuy offers. Just as they do at the other three big chains, Asda takes 25% off purchases of six or more wines, any mix, for defined periods.

In the longer term, let's hope Asda will resume determined competition in the own-label wine market. I fully realise the company has had distractions at corporate level, what with being sold off by Wal-mart following an aborted merger with Sainsbury's, and now owned by an enterprise devoted to petrol stations and forecourt shops.

RED WINES

Asda

ARGENTINA

9 Viñalba Reserve Malbec 2021   £8.50
Good to find this serious Mendoza wine at Asda, at a keen
price – it's usually a tenner upwards. Silkily oaked cassis fruit
with plummy depths, trademark roasty savours of malbec on
nose and palate; 14.5% alcohol. Viñalba is among Argentina's
winemaking elite, and a name to look out for at all levels.

AUSTRALIA

9 Extra Special Barossa Valley Shiraz 2021   £8.00
Full-on but artfully contrived black-fruit monster combining
rich, spicy, regional super-ripeness (it's sunny in the Barossa)
with a sort of mineral poise that makes this one stand out from
what is a very large crowd; 14.5% alcohol. I got mine for just
£5.25 on a two-level promo.

10 Wirra Wirra Church Block
Cabernet Sauvignon-Shiraz-Merlot 2020   £13.00
This famous McLaren Vale classic has been in production for
50 years, and is new to Asda in 2023. Better late than never.
It's simply gorgeous: lavish blackcurrant and blackberry
juiciness, poised cushiony spicing, and I agree with the maker's
claim to suggestions of cedar, black olive and dried thyme;
14.5% alcohol. In the round this is a world-class wine, a flag-
flyer for Australia and a welcome signal that Asda still has a
true wine agenda.

CHILE

8 Nice Drop of Malbec 2021   £4.25
From Asda's budget range of a dozen or so different varietals
all under a fiver, my pick is this decent focused savoury-ripe
choc-and-berry mouthfiller; 13% alcohol. Nice bargain drop.

RED WINES

CHILE

8 **Extra Special Carmenère 2022** £7.25

The Colchagua Valley has a good name for carmenère wines, well-liked for their deep maroon colour ('carmine' as in the varietal name) and juicy succulence; this fits the model: focused black fruits firmed with tannin and suggestions of spicy-chocolatey richness; 14% alcohol.

FRANCE

8 **Baron Augustin 2021** £5.75

Merlot-based mellow generic claret with an impressive if irrelevant image of a grand château on the label. It really does impress with its forward, even creamy, fruit; 13% alcohol. Proper Bordeaux wine around the five-quid mark used to be a no-go area, but there are now hopeful signs.

8 **Extra Special Plan de Dieu Côtes du Rhône Villages 2020** £8.75

Classy CdR delivering warm-south savours of baked, spicy blackberry-compote to match the hearty flavours of duck and saucisson, ideally included in a beany cassoulet; wine to tempt you; 14.5% alcohol.

8 **Extra Special Château Le Boscq 2016** £13.00

Very proper claret from the Médoc AC which has equivocal status under the Bordeaux ranking system of *cru bourgeois* but there's noble intent here: generously ripened blackcurrant-sour-cherry fruit of elegant weight and mature roundness; 13.5% alcohol.

ITALY

8 **Extra Special Montepulciano d'Abruzzo 2021** £6.00

Perennial bargain from Italy's east midlands on fine form in this vintage, juicy with cherry-bramble fruits and appreciable weight; clean edge, stimulating pasta wine; 13.5% alcohol.

RED WINES

ITALY

8 **Burdizzo Chianti Riserva 2019** £8.25

Poised violet-scented sour-cherry fruit Chianti in the best tradition at an untypically reasonable price – especially for a *riserva* wine, aged in oak casks for a couple of years to add slinkiness to the juicy fruits; 12.5% alcohol.

PORTUGAL

8 **Bodacious Red 2020** £7.25

The name of this raging-bull-themed brand, I gather, is a portmanteau of bold and audacious and consequently apposite to the nature of the wine, a blend of cabernet sauvignon with aragonez and castelão, varieties local to the region of origin, Alentejo. It's big with berry fruits, juicy and vigorous with trademark clove and cinnamon spicing, full and satisfying; 13.5% alcohol. Last time I wrote about this wine, the price was £8.00. No bull!

8 **Extra Special Douro 2021** £7.50

Made not as usually by a Port producer but by big-brand outfit Falua of Alentejo, this is a nevertheless convincing table wine with the heady cassis and mint aromas of the fortified model and good intensity of matching blackberry-pruny fruit, plumped with oak contact; 13.5% alcohol.

SPAIN

8 **Extra Special Old Vine Garnacha 2022** £6.75

Really quite potent mouthfilling newly-squished berry-fruit compote of juicy flavours tasting savoury and complete at a very modest price; 14.5% alcohol.

9 **Extra Special Rioja Gran Reserva**
Marques del Norte 2016 £12.50

Dark aromas of rose-petal, sweet vanilla and blackcurrant from this slinky maturing wine from excellent El Coto bodega foretell luscious cassis-and-cream fruit in elegant balance, clean edge of acidity; 14% alcohol.

PINK WINES

8 **Extra Special Malbec Rosé 2022**   £7.15
The restrained shell-pink colour is echoed in the delicate strawberry-citrus-rose-petal scent and crisp corresponding fruit, pretty dry and very fresh with reassuring balance; 13.5% alcohol.

8 **Le Cellier de Saint Louis Coteaux du Varois en Provence Rosé 2022**   £8.00
From the Var, a beautiful but less-discovered corner of Provence, this has a fine delicate pale-coppery colour, fresh fruit-blossom aromas and red soft summer fruit savours, dry, brisk and refreshing; 13% alcohol. It's a bargain by Provence standards. When I last reported on this wine, in 2021, the price was £8.50. How interesting!

8 **Viña Albali Tempranillo Rosado 2022**   £5.50
Mega-brand it may be, but this exuberant magenta party pink from the wine lake that is La Mancha delivers generous but brisk strawberry-cassis fruit, soft but not sweet textures and refreshment as well as fun; 11.5% alcohol.

WHITE WINES

8 **Yalumba y Series Viognier 2021**   £7.95
Yalumba in the Barossa is the oldest family-owned winery (est 1859) in Oz and makes wines of character. This dry but lush pure varietal has the expected honeysuckly aroma of the viognier and a delightfully harmonious nectar-citrus uplifting fruit; 13.5% alcohol.

Asda

WHITE WINES

AUSTRALIA

8 Extra Special Chardonnay 2021 £8.00

This rather luscious Barossa Valley wine recalls the 'buttery' confections of early oak-chipped Aussie brands, but the richness is balanced here by a very contemporary citrus twang to complement the blanched-nut creaminess; fun, fresh and 13.5% alcohol.

CHILE

8 La Corriente Sauvignon Blanc 2022 £7.00

Very approachable softer-style Chilean sauvignon with ripe fruit-salad savours as well as the grape's trademark green apple and seagrass twang with a lifting lime-grapefruit acidity; 12.5% alcohol. Eye-catching label, attractive dry wine.

FRANCE

8 Extra Special Côtes de Gascogne 2021 £7.25

This smart package from Gascony delivers the expected message: crisp-apple ripeness with sunny peachy fleshiness nicely tied up with zesty citrus acidity. The wines of this region of southwest France used to go mostly into distilling armagnac; now they are among the nation's most interesting for everyday drinking; 11.5% alcohol.

8 Paul Mas Chardonnay 2022 £8.00

A new one to me from Paul Mas of Mediterranean France, prolific producer of quaily wines for most of the UK supermarkets. This is a straight ripe-apple dry wine with a discreet sweet vanilla background and healthy notes of white peach, skilfully tied up with a brisk citrus acidity; 13.5% alcohol.

8 Extra Special Vouvray Chenin Blanc 2021 £8.00

The town and AC of Vouvray is HQ to the chenin blanc grape in the Loire Valley, making delectable white wines ranging in style from dry to very sweet. This one is off-dry, fresh from the chenin's juicy orchard-fruit influence and enriched with the honeysuckle aromas and candied fruit of its sweeter side; fascinating, versatile and delicious; 13% alcohol.

WHITE WINES

FRANCE

9 **Extra Special Touraine Sauvignon Blanc 2022** £9.00
Zingy river-pebble-fresh green-fruit sauvignon in the best
Loire Valley tradition and thrillingly good; 13% alcohol.
The Touraine appellation incorporates the world's grandest
sauvignon spots, Sancerre and Pouilly-sur-Loire, where the
wines closely resemble a generic such as this, at twice the price.

9 **Trimbach Riesling 2020** £17.50
If you're a follower of Alsace you'll already know that
Trimbach, established in 1626, is among the region's top names
for riesling wines. Here's a fine example at what I promise is a
fair price: golden-looking and golden-tasting with wild aromas
of apple, pear, nectarine even pineapple, distant wood smoke,
lemon lift, ripe pungency and racy freshness; it's dry wine but
weighty and exotic; a match for the most challenging menus;
13% alcohol. I got mine at £14 on promo.

GERMANY

10 **Dr L Riesling 2021** £7.00
Fragrant moselle from fabled Bernkastel-based winemaker Dr
Ernst Loosen (it's pronounced "LOHzen") is scintillating in
this vintage. Apple characteristics – both crisp green and sweet
red – light up the aromas and savours in an elusively honeyed
dry wine of crisp freshness and just 8.5% alcohol. Classic racy
riesling at a bewilderingly low price.

ITALY

8 **Extra Special Fiano Terre Siciliane 2021** £6.75
Fiano is a grape variety native to southern Italy and cultivated
for wine in the region for more than 2,000 years. Take a sniff
of this sunnily perfumed Sicilian dry white and you might just
be carried back to the time when appreciative Romans called
it *apianum* on account of the grape's irresistible appeal to bees
(apis in Latin). In harmony with the wine's crisp, nectarine-
citrus freshness is a true nectary plumpness that gives it a
classical balance; 12.5% alcohol.

WHITE WINES

8 Extra Special Soave Classico 2022 £7.25

Citrus-blossom nose, hint of green in the lemon-gold colour and a tangy white fruit slyly revealing a blanched-almond richness in this likeable and typical Veronese fresh and dry wine; 12.5% alcohol. Good price, safe bet.

8 Tukituki Sauvignon Blanc 2022 £8.50

Zesty granny smith apple is evoked by the scent of this limey-seagrassy and characteristically vivacious Marlborough wine called after the Maori word for 'smash'; 12.5% alcohol.

9 The Ned Pinot Grigio 2022 £9.50

Don't expect anything like the vacuous vino of Italy's Veneto PG from this. The Ned is far more elevated – named after a high peak in the Marlborough region's Waihopai Valley, whose foothills host the vineyards for a famous sauvignon blanc as well as this remarkable Kiwi spin on the pinot gris. The colour is very subtly pink, because the juice has steeped briefly with the grape's coppery skin. You get a gently pungent, smoky savour in the crisp apple-pear-citrus fruit and sublime freshness and vivacity; 13.5% alcohol.

8 The Wine Atlas Feteasca Regala 2021 £6.25

A relic of Asda's largely deleted Wine Atlas range of own-labels from around the world, this remains a fascinating bargain. From Romania's indigenous Feteasca grape, it's softly lush, just shy of dry, with distinctive nectarine-pineapple notes, freshness and citrus twang; 11.5% alcohol.

WHITE WINES

SOUTH AFRICA

🍷 **8**   **Extra Special Chenin Blanc 2021**   £7.00
Barrel-fermented dry wine convincingly marrying trademark chenin blanc floral aroma and peachy fruit with lemon twang to make a finely balanced whole; 13.5% alcohol.

🍷 **8**   **Extra Special Sauvignon Blanc 2022**   £7.75
Cheery green-fruit and grassy-fresh sauvignon in the Cape manner; tangy grapefruit twist and crisp close; 12.5% alcohol. The price of this wine increased dramatically during the year – from just £6 when I tasted it – but it's still a good buy.

SPAIN

🍷 **9**   **Extra Special Palacio de Vivera Rueda 2022**   £6.00
Fine pure verdejo savours of grassiness, sharp-apple and lemon twang in this nicely coloured dry wine from rightly revered Rueda region of Castille high country; 13% alcohol. Very keen value.

🍷 **8**   **Extra Special Albariño Rias Baixas 2022**   £9.75
From northern Spain's Atlantic shore, a particularly breezy and tangy refresher of lush green fruits and limey acidity; poised in savour and finely balanced; 12.5% alcohol.

The Co-op

First things first. It's now called The Co-op, and not The Co-operative. Look at the fascia on your local branch – you do probably have one, as there are 2,400 Co-op stores throughout the realm – and you'll see what I mean.

There's no sign, happily, of any concomitant abbreviation of the Co-op's wine selection. At the tasting this year I was impressed by introductions to the 'Irresistible' range such as the Co-op's first Swiss wine, a particularly perky non-vintage red called La Courbe, and a white Mâcon-Villages from the 2022 vintage strongly suggesting that's a very good year in Burgundy (after a miserable 2021).

Fairtrade wines persist as a mainstay of the Co-op range and the ethically oriented retailer is certainly a mainstay of this great scheme to support the workforces of wonderful wineries like La Riojana in Argentina and Vergelegen in South Africa, the latter a very grand old estate that has only lately (to my knowledge) joined the movement and brings Fairtrade firmly into the premier division.

In keeping with the general move in the direction of discounting of wine in supermarkets, the Co-op this year has for the first time launched across-the-range deals including multibuy savings on purchases of three bottles at a time. You get more of a discount if you're a Co-op member and show your card (just as you would at Tesco with a Clubcard).

The Co-op will continue to discount individual wines, as they always have, and on a good day you might find there are double discounts to be had.

One day, I hope the Co-op will get into home deliveries of wine via an online service, because among those 2,400 outlets there are only a few hundred that stock a really wide choice from the overall range. In the meantime, a reminder that you can look online to find your nearest Co-op stockist for all the wines featured in the following pages.

RED WINES

ARGENTINA

🍷 **9** **Co-op Irresistible Fairtrade Organic Malbec 2020 £8.00**
This has, I think, mellowed since I tasted it at the Co-op in 2022, and it's deliciously savoury with juicy black fruits, and grippy at the finish; 13% alcohol. Writing this after the 2023 Co-op tasting I was only sorry to discover later that this vintage hadn't yet sold out. It deserves to.

🍷 **9** **Don David Malbec 2022** **£9.50**
Luxury oaked wine made under the Fairtrade scheme. Opaque colour, silky expensive aromas and fruits with malbec trademarks of warmth and new leather, spice and succulence; 14% alcohol. It's a lot of wine for the money.

AUSTRALIA

🍷 **8** **Wild Lands 2021** **£8.50**
New brand from Banrock Station, the Murray River outpost of global wine giant Accolade who seem anxious to prove their eco credentials. So, Wild branding, sensitive vineyard and winery practices, the lot. This Bordeaux-style blend comes out of it well: wholesome cabernet-merlot combo, brightly delicious, intensified with oak contact and nicely poised; 14% alcohol.

🍷 **8** **Vandenberg Shiraz Cabernet 2021** **£8.00**
Blood-red Limestone Coast fruit bomb staying safely short of overripeness and turning out healthily weighted and balanced. I warmed to what is just the kind of red you need for winter nights; 14.5% alcohol.

CHILE

🍷 **9** **Co-op Irresistible Carmenère 2022** **£8.00**
The strong inky colour is matched by intense ripe dark minty-blackcurrant fruit, plumped by time in oak casks, all in healthy balance; 14% alcohol. In the bold new package, a smart buy at a good price.

RED WINES

🍷 8 Co-op Irresistible Pais 2022 £7.00

Pais is said to have been the first vitis vinifera (wine grape) from Europe to be planted in Chile centuries ago, and it has long been central to the country's bulk-wine industry. Here's a new spin: organically grown oak-matured Pais in the Co-op's smartly updated Irresistible range; it's middling in colour and weight, distinctively focused in its lively juicy red fruits, nicely balanced with a clean edge; 13.5% alcohol.

**🍷 9 Co-op Irresistible Casablanca
Valley Pinot Noir 2022** £8.50

Gold-standard New World pinot aligning full-on ripeness of cherry-raspberry fruit with earthy warmth and intensity, carrying the long flavours through to a lovely defined finish; 14% alcohol. Perfect poultry and game partner. Or maybe a sausage.

**🍷 9 Co-op Fairtrade Chilean
Red Blend 2022 3-ltr box** £21.74

Essayed for an appearance of Channel 4's *Sunday Brunch* show, this is seriously good, and priced at the equivalent of £5.44 per 75cl (as in bottle-size). I asked the people at the Co-op to suggest a box I might try, so credit must go to them (thank you, Lauren) for this revelation. The blend is anonymous but it's full of life: jewel-like colour, frisky berry aroma with a hint of healthy stalkiness, bright, juicy, pleasingly raspy flavours, finishing dry and clean; will chill well, like Beaujolais; 12.5% alcohol.

RED WINES

FRANCE

10 Château Vieux Manoir 2020 £8.50
To my mind the best vintage to date of this perennial Co-op exclusive from the Entre-Deux-Mers backwater of Bordeaux. Humble of origin it may be, but it's a big, full claret from one third cabernet sauvignon and two of merlot, abounding in brambly-cherry-cassis vigour, warmly ripe (14.5% alcohol) and well-balanced in its acidity; true bargain. One carp: a horrible polymer 'cork'.

9 Château Capitoul 2021 £8.50
Roasty spicy black fruits keenly edged with trim acidity mark this handsome Languedoc blend of syrah, grenache and carignan; back-label's suggested match to duck dishes makes sense, as would a sausage or two; 13% alcohol.

8 Doudet Naudin Pinot Noir 2022 £9.25
Good intensity in this Languedoc wine gives the cherry-berry fruit firmness and persistence – a relishable variation on the pinot theme; 13% alcohol.

9 Carius Cairanne Cru des Côtes du Rhône 2019 £10.00
Immediately appealing, smartly presented top-drawer CdR: darkly magnificent colour, aroma and fruit in the best regional tradition, silky and warmly spicy, probably benefiting from its relative maturity; 2019 was a great harvest, and the launch vintage for Cairanne's newly won status as an individual appellation on the Rhône's expanding AC ladder, along with the likes of pricy Gigondas and Vacqueyras. Perfectly balanced classic and one of my CdRs of the year; 14.5% alcohol.

RED WINES

FRANCE

🍷 9 | **Château de Ruth Côtes du Rhône Villages Ste Cécile 2021** £10.00

Substantial weight and savour in this earthy-piquant rather opulent (though unoaked) single-estate wine from the Vinsobres *cru* but somehow outside the official appellation; 14.5% alcohol.

🍷 9 | **Jean-Jacques Girard Savigny-lès-Beaune 2020** £20.50

The first Jean Girard to cultivate a vineyard at Savigny, a treasure of a village next to the city of Beaune, got started in 1529, and there's still a Girard, Vincent, at it today. This is a fine red burgundy worthy of the name, unexpectedly deep beetroot in colour with a lush summer-red-fruit pinot fragrance, elegant middle weight and silkiness edged with friendly tannin; 13% alcohol. By burgundy standards, the price looks a gift.

ITALY

🍷 8 | **Marchesini Piemonte Rosso 2022** £7.25

Eyecatchingly labelled generic from Piedmont is a blend of the local Barolo grape, nebbiolo, with barbera and merlot. And it shows in the friendly rose-petal aroma, light but structured red fruits with coffee notes and brambly bounce; 13% alcohol.

🍷 8 | **Sannio Janare Aglianico Selezione 2020** £8.00

New arrival of a wine I've seen elsewhere at £12. Aglianico is a rightly admired grape of the Campania in southern Italy, making dark and grippy food reds that balance sweet ripeness with spicy earthiness; this nicely fits the formula; 13% alcohol.

🍷 9 | **Vanita Negroamaro 2021** £8.95

Perennial from Puglia with its unmissably rococo label is as delightful as ever in this vintage: chocolate and cherry light up the nose and fruit, which streams distinct prune and blackberry savours, is briskly edged with natural tannin; 13.5% alcohol.

RED WINES

ITALY

Y **9** **Palladino Molise Biferno Riserva 2018** £9.50
New vintage of last year's 10-scoring 2017 is up in price but still delicious. It's a blend of montepulciano grapes with aglianico, which combine into a lusciously ripe whole with sun-baked black-berry fruit savours, sweet highlights and notes of clove and mint made sleek with oak contact; 13% alcohol.

Y **8** **Tenuta Trerose Vino Nobile di Montepulciano Riserva 2018** £13.00
Slick intense sour-cherry-raspberry super-Chianti; its maturity brings creaminess and lingering piquant fruit with notions of tobacco and mint amid the richness; 14.5% alcohol.

NEW ZEALAND

Y **8** **Grove Mill Pinot Noir 2021** £10.50
Kiwi pinot noir has prospered much less in the gobal market than all that NZ sauvignon blanc. Maybe it's that it doesn't rival French – and particularly Burgundian – pinot for interest or value. But I like this one. It's poised with a proper hit of sunny strawberry-cherry pinot fruit, earthiness, gentle spice and grip, 13.5% alcohol and a message: this is pinot unlike others.

SOUTH AFRICA

Y **10** **Vergelegen Cabernet Sauvignon Merlot Fairtrade 2019** £10.00
I'm not letting this one get away. It was my top red wine under £10 in last year's edition and even with the price hike still scores top – and in the same vintage, 2019, which I retasted in summer 2023 and loved every bit as much as last time round. If anything it's even more rounded, silky and lingeringly delicious; 14% alcohol. Ignore back-label advice that it's a match for pizza; it's much better than that. A classic Sunday roast will suit, or for true connoisseurs, a sausage feast.

RED WINES

SPAIN

🍷 8 **Co-op Garnacha 2022** £6.75
Brambly picnic red from humble but often good-value Campo de Borja region; delivers firm fruit in wholesome balance; 14% alcohol.

🍷 8 **Jumilla Castillo de Zalin Monastrell 2021** £8.50
Solid new vintage of this recent organic addition to the Co-op's Spanish offering, it has spicy sinew through the juicy hedgerow black fruits and a good tight finish – a nice match for rich meaty offering, especially, dare I say it, sausage dishes; 14% alcohol.

🍷 8 **Davida No Added Sulphites Garnacha 2022** £8.00
The phrase No Added Sulphites really is boldly emblazoned on the front label of this righteous Navarra wine. On the positive side, it has healthy, supple black-fruit texture and savour in the admirable Navarra style and 14% alcohol. The vaunted absence of sulphur is unnoticeable.

SWITZERLAND

🍷 8 **Co-op Irresistible La Courbe** £11.00
Perhaps it's a gimmick to boost the Co-op's newly revamped Irresistible range, but the introduction of a Swiss wine is more than a mere gesture. The main reason wines from Switzerland are sparse abroad is that they're so good nearly all are consumed by the Swiss. Here's an example: a sleek, juicy, ripe-berry, easy-weighted anytime red with poise and a trim finish; 12.5% alcohol. It's a blend of Gamaret grapes (a Swiss-developed offshoot of Gamay, the grape of Beaujolais) with pinot noir from more than one vintage.

PINK WINES

8 · B. Ink Rosé 2022 £8.50

AUSTRALIA

B. Ink is a new brand by global wine giant Accolade, from one of its Australian properties, Grant Burge. This is a decent rosé, party-frock colour, ripe on nose and palate with cherry, strawberry and redcurrant but brisk, fresh and clean at the close; 13.5% alcohol.

8 · La Petite Laurette du Midi Rosé 2022 £9.85

FRANCE

Midi – informal name for Mediterranean France from the Pyrenees to the Italian Alps – rarely gets a mention on wine labels, but here's a plump, pleasing pink that does it the honour. Pale shell colour, delicate red-fruit aroma and savour, nicely contrived acidity; 12.5% alcohol. Sensible price.

8 · Château La Négly La Natice Rosé 2022 £13.00

This smartly presented Languedoc wine from a rated estate is a pleasing salmon colour, crisp and tangy, full of blossomy, juicy interest and smartly balanced; 13% alcohol. This is proper rosé, at a price.

8 · Tommasi Chiaretto Rosé 2022 £10.50

ITALY

Chiaretto is the name for the pink wines of Bardolino, the Lake Garda DOC known for red wines so pale they can themselves be mistaken for rosé. This one is very pale indeed, but full of interest – red cherry ripeness bouncing along with zesty minerality; very dry; 12% alcohol.

8 · Irresistible Solo Rosé 2022 £8.25

SPAIN

Pale-petal coloured all-garnacha from the Campo de Borja region; generously ripe with summer fruit and artfully balanced; 13.5% alcohol.

PINK WINES

SPAIN

🍷 8 **Ramón Bilbao Rioja Rosado 2022** £9.75

The good pale onion-skin colour attracts the eye to this garnacha-based pink Rioja, which successfully rivals the grenache rosé styles of Provence (westwards beyond the Pyrenees) for flavour and freshness, in this case at a competitive price; 12.5% alcohol.

WHITE WINES

AUSTRALIA

🍷 8 **Wild Lands 2022** £7.50

This is a new brand (to me) of Banrock Station, a big-scale producer of the Murray River in South Australia, owned by mega wine corp Accolade. In keeping with current signalling, Wild Lands wines are made responsibly, sold in lightweight bottles and so on. But here's the thing: this is good by any lights: an unlikely mix of chardonnay, fiano, colombard and verdelho grapes coalesces into an intriguingly fresh, eager and relishable dry wine of evident quality; 13% alcohol.

🍷 8 **The Hidden Sea Chardonnay 2022** £10.00

Cheerfully retro Limestone Coast oaked wine living up to the marine theme with saline freshness as well as traditional Aussie upfront ripe orchard fruit; 12.5% alcohol.

FRANCE

🍷 8 **Maison du Vin Côtes de Gascogne 2021** £6.50

Value wine; dry but herbaceous in the likeable Gascon manner with summery orchard-fruit freshness and a citrus lift; 11.5% alcohol.

🍷 8 **Château de la Petite Giraudière**
Muscadet de Sèvre et Maine Sur Lie 2021 £8.75

Nice example of the Loire-estuary oyster-matcher; crisp, almost prickly, with green-apple-lemon zing and authentic leesy flavours; 12% alcohol. Not too sharp, and reasonably priced.

WHITE WINES

9 **Co-op Irresistible Mâcon-Villages**
Chardonnay 2022 £10.50
It seems *de trop* to mention chardonnay on the label, as all
white Mâconnais must be made solely from this grape, but this
is a particularly good chardonnay, by top co-operative Cave
de Lugny, so there: stony-lemony-ripe-apple scent and savour,
sunny ripeness, brisk, clean and typical; 13% alcohol.

9 **Silène Chardonnay Limoux 2021** £10.00
The front label is just a cut-out image of the head of Silenus,
an ancient Roman wine god. But don't be deterred: this is a
divinely good mineral-sherbetty-sumptuous pure chardonnay
made by producer Jean-Claude Mas in the appellation of
Limoux (mostly known for sparkling wines, but also quite
special for still) – in deepest south west France; 13.5% alcohol.

8 **G de Château Guiraud 2022** £15.50
From a very grand Sauternes estate whose sumptuous sweet
wines cost £50 upwards, a rather lovely Bordeaux Blanc Sec
from the same vines – sauvignon and semillon – but picked a
lot earlier in the ripening season; traces of richness but fresh,
tangy and uplifting; 13% alcohol.

8 **Kleine Kapelle Pinot Grigio 2022** £7.50
From the Pfalz region of the Rhine, a likeable spin on Italy's
perpetual PG phenomenon. Easy sweet-apple fruit of healthy,
natural freshness, and at a keen price; 11.5% alcohol.

8 **Von Kesselstatt Mosel Riesling 2021** £14.00
Grapey and racy unflashy moselle from a noble producer; quite
dry but not without a peachy richness to add nuance; fine
aperitif; 11.5% alcohol.

WHITE WINES

ITALY

8 **Verdicchio dei Castelli di Jesi 2022** £7.65
A trace of petillance in this herbaceous Marches classic gives it extra appeal as a refreshing summery dry white Italian wine of character; 13.5% alcohol.

NEW ZEALAND

8 **Grove Mill Sauvignon Blanc 2022** £9.00
The assertive grassy-nettly first flavour of this classy Wairau Valley (Marlborough) wine gives an immediate lift to the senses, following up with long lushness of fruit; 12% alcohol. Price is up from £7 for the excellent 2021 vintage last year.

8 **The Ned Sauvignon Blanc 2022** £10.50
Now-iconic leading brand named after a mountain peak of the Waihopai valley in Marlborough (although the author of this book never tires of equivocally denying any connection), it's as good as ever in this vintage: bold, nettly textbook Kiwi sauvignon with freshness and zeal; 13% alcohol.

8 **Vavasour Sauvignon Blanc 2022** £12.25
Ripeness amid the grassy-gooseberry greenness gives ponderable savour to this rather ritzy Marlborough wine; 12.5% alcohol.

SOUTH AFRICA

8 **Cape Point Sauvignon Semillon Fairtrade 2022** £8.00
The semillon share is just one seventh of the whole but the ripe tropical lushness comes clearly through to give the grassy green main constituent a lot of extra interest. Really successful blend at a good price, and Fairtrade into the bargain; 12.5% alcohol.

SPARKLING WINES

ENGLAND

9 Co-op Irresistible Eight Acres Sparkling Rosé   £19.50
English sparkling wines are now booming and the Co-op has been an early adopter, especially of the redoubtable Balfour estate in Kent, whence comes this delicately pink and vivacious Champagne-grape blend with its bready richness, strawberry trace and enlivening freshness; 11.5% alcohol.

8 Maison du Vin Crémant de Loire   £11.75
Very busily fizzing in its creamy mousse and in its freshness and lively orchard-fruit flavours, a fine party wine from the Loire's indigenous chenin blanc grape with added chardonnay and black-skinned cabernet franc; 11.5% alcohol.

FRANCE

10 Les Pionniers Champagne Brut   £22.75
Consistently delicious house Champagne made for the Co-op by Piper Heidsieck and named to commemorate the Pioneers of Rochdale who set up the first co-operative retail movement back in 1844 – an inauguration always worthy of celebration. I very much like the lemon-meringue-pie aroma of this lively, creamily sparkling non-vintage wine with its elegant balance of ripe-apple fruit and tangy citrus zing; 12% alcohol. Top marks for value. In spite of other supermarket own-label Champagnes moving up in price of late, this bargain is cheaper than it was a decade ago.

Lidl

At last, good news of wine-department developments at Lidl. After a lengthy period of abstinence, I have finally managed to get to one of their press tastings to catch up not just with the range but with my old friend and Master of Wine Richard Bampfield.

Mr Bampfield has a unique profile as the face of Lidl wine. As 'our independent lead taster' he plays a big role in the selection of wines for the periodical 'Wine Tour' collections that are featured through the year, and rates each of them on a scale of 80 to 100 for quality. His scores – and his portrait photos – are prominently displayed in the stores.

Lidl is the only mass-retailer to promote its wines in this way, and it's clearly working. Many of the Wine Tour wines are interesting and good value. But they cannot, sadly, feature in the pages of this guide because by the time it gets into print each year, the wines have been replaced. As they say at Lidl: When it's gone, it's gone.

Lidl does of course have a 'core' list of wines stocked year-round, and I have long wished that this very limited and strangely static selection might suddenly take off into wider fields than it has to date. And that's where the good news comes in. I have now tasted sufficient current core-range wines to be able to offer 30 commendations in the following pages.

Among them is a sprinkling of Deluxe wines. You might recognise the brand as Lidl's premium designation – familiar from all sorts of food products. Well, it's now being adopted for a new range to be added to the old regulars. I fervently hope Deluxe wines as a range will expand exponentially in the near future.

RED WINES

AUSTRALIA

⚱ 8 **Deluxe Barossa Valley Shiraz 2021**   £6.79
Pungently ripe bumper baked blueberry savours in this easy-weighted barbecue red just this side of cooked; really quite wholesome and tidy at the finish; 14% alcohol. The price is definitely an attraction.

CHILE

⚱ 8 **Deluxe Carmenère Gran Reserva 2021**   £7.99
Handsomely coloured and generously oaked baked-red-fruit food wine (good with pasta as well as meat menus); rounded and satisfying; 14% alcohol.

FRANCE

⚱ 8 **Bordeaux 2021**   £4.79
Generic claret; a plump blackberry merlot with focus and heft, healthily ripe and balanced; defined tannin finish; 13.5% alcohol. Jolly good effort at the price.

⚱ 9 **Pinot Noir Vin de France 2022**   £5.79
This is good: poised cherry-raspberry pinot of bright hue, juicy aromas and wholesomely earthy classic cherry-raspberry fruit, finishing brisk; 12.5% alcohol. Chill for warm-weather occasions.

⚱ 9 **Bordeaux Supérieur 2021**   £5.99
Impressive full blackcurranty and grippy claret that tastes as it should – and a lot better than I am accustomed to at this price level. A delightful bargain; 13.5% alcohol.

⚱ 8 **Saint-Emilion Grand Cru 2020**   £14.99
Anonymous but proper right-bank Bordeaux that does honour to the famed appellation, already showing full, round minty-blackberry fruit with cedar and spice, a shade of liquorice and ripening tannins; not cheap but fair value; 14% alcohol. Lidl suggest drinking it within two years but I'd leave it another two years before opening. Should develop well.

RED WINES

FRANCE

🍷 8 **Châteauneuf du Pape Les Paroisses 2021** £16.99
A handsome-looking package that has the customary oaked mélange of black and red fruit flavours, warm spice and intensity that set this grand appellation above its humbler Rhône neighbours, and it's already quite rounded and mellow; 14.5% alcohol.

ITALY

🍷 8 **Maestro de Pigo Primitivo di Manduria 2021** £6.49
A German bottling helpfully labelled 'Trocken' – meaning dry. Intriguing spicy-baked-plum aromas are followed up by savoury red and blackberry fruits in this middleweight Puglian pasta red which does indeed finish dry; 14% alcohol.

PORTUGAL

🍷 8 **Azinhaga de Ouro Reserva Tinto 2021** £5.99
This Douro Valley table wine, made from the same grape variteies that go into Port, has been a Lidl regular for ever, and this is the best vintage I've tasted. It has the rich black berry ripeness of the fortified wine, but in an elegantly weighted body of fruit, nicely balanced to finish dry and brisk and with a healthy 13.5% alcohol.

SOUTH AFRICA

🍷 9 **Deluxe Coastal Region Fairtrade Pinotage 2021** £5.49
The colour's a sort of dark magenta, unusually light for pinotage, and the nose is friendly, naturally piquant with the ID-kit tarriness of the grape present but not dominant. The flavour in the mouth is equally amenable, juicy, clean, wholesome and definitely pinotage; distinctive, really well-made wine from a Fairtrade producer at a very fair price; 14% alcohol.

RED WINES

SPAIN

🍷 **9** **Cepa Lebrel Rioja Crianza 2019** £5.49
The bold new labelling for this Lidl perennial heralds the best vintage I can recall: cassis-vanilla perfume, defined dark-fruit flavours with vigour and oak-imparted richness, working harmoniously; serious 'nursery' Rioja at an incomprehensibly low price; 14% alcohol.

PINK WINES

FRANCE

🍷 **8** **Chevalier de Fauvert Syrah Pays d'Oc Rosé 2022** £5.49
Shell pink, soft but not flabby delicate wine with alpine-strawberry notes in the bright fruit, fresh and friendly; 12.5% alcohol.

🍷 **8** **Pinot Noir Rosé Pays d'Oc 2021** £5.99
Pale salmon colour, plenty of cherry-strawberry pink fruit with a note, even, of pink grapefruit, so nicely tangy and refreshingly dry; 12.5% alcohol.

ITALY

🍷 **7** **Ca' del Lago Rosa delle Dame 2022** £5.99
Salmon pink, positively potent, dry rosé from the Trevenezie region of north east Italy; crisp redcurrant-raspberry fruit and forward lemon acidity; 12% alcohol.

WHITE WINES

AUSTRALIA

🍷 **8** **Deluxe Limestone Coast Chardonnay 2021** £6.79
Strong-tasting, near-viscous bumper-ripe unoaked dry textbook Aussie chardonnay – an outdoor kind of wine to partner prawns off the barbie and all sorts of spicy menus; 13% alcohol.

WHITE WINES

9 **Chevalier de Fauvert Sauvignon Blanc 2022** £4.75
Catchy green edge to the fruit on first taste, an unmistakable sauvignon with the full ID of green pepper, grassiness and gooseberry pizzazz; very likeable bargain from the Languedoc; 12% alcohol.

8 **Chevalier de Fauvert Chardonnay 2022** £4.75
Wholesome sweet-apple pure varietal from Languedoc with plumpness and a tinge of spearmint and lemon lift; decent party dry white bargain; 12% alcohol.

8 **Picpoul de Pinet Le Rocher Saint Victor 2022** £8.29
Lots of gold colour and full, slightly saline, green fruit in the approved Picpoul manner but quite light in weight; refreshing Mediterranean dry white worthy of the name; 12.5% alcohol.

8 **Chablis 2022** £14.99
This standard-issue Chablis has attractive colour, crisp apple aroma and fruit with detectable struck-match minerality of this famous and expensive appellation; good leesy weight and easy acidity; 12.5% alcohol.

10 **Brauneberger Kurfürstlay Riesling Mosel 2021** £5.29
This transcendent moselle is a pantheon of virtues: fresh dry (it's labelled *feinherb* meaning near-dry) aperitif wine with scintillating lemon perfume, wildly fresh apple-juicy classic riesling fruit, racy yet lingering, tingling and lush, just 10.5% alcohol and yet spot on for residual sugar, and priced at a fraction of its worth. A marvel and maybe a signpost to what more Lidl could do with the wines of its own origins.

WHITE WINES

🍷 9 **Markus Molitor Sauvignon Blanc 2021**   £9.99
Totally out of the box, a sauvignon blanc from the Mosel, it has hallmark snappy green-pepper zest, grassy lushness and a certain minerality; 12% alcohol. Intriguing choice for Lidl from a recognised grower on their home turf. More, please.

🍷 7 **Soave Classico 2020**   £3.99
Unexpectedly weighty rendering of the renowned Verona dry white; brisk orchard-fruit aroma and matching fruit with just a suggestion of nuttiness; 11.5% alcohol.

🍷 9 **Botte Conti Pecorino Terre di Chieti 2021**   £5.99
Prickly-fresh dry Abruzzo wine delivering masses of crisp orchard fruit savour with healthy resiny structure, really quite delicious, very Italian and a versatile food matcher; 12% alcohol. This is a fine example of the popular pecorino style (the grape is unconnected to *pecora*, Italian for sheep but there are always sheep on the label), and at a keen price; 12% alcohol.

🍷 8 **Gavi 2021**   £7.49
Big flavours in this generously coloured food wine in comfortable balance between orchard fruits and citrus twang with suggestions of exotic fruits in the mix; 12% alcohol.

🍷 8 **Deluxe Awatere Valley Sauvignon Blanc 2022**   £8.49
Peapod and passionfruit pop up in this easy-to-like Marlborough wine, gentle on acidity, strong on freshness and zest; textbook Kiwi sauvignon at a competitive price; 12% alcohol.

WHITE WINES

PORTUGAL

🍷 **8** **Portal do Minho Vinho Verde 2022** £5.49

Water white and shy of aroma, this quirky vinho verde exhibits very little 'prickle' but nevertheless has an impressive lemony appeal and is most unusually dry; 10% alcohol. At home in Portugal, vv – red as well as white – is extremely dry and 'green' in style but export brands tend to be sweetened for the UK and US.

SOUTH AFRICA

🍷 **8** **Deluxe Paarl Chenin Blanc 2022** £6.99

Fairtrade wine – very glad to see that in Lidl – at the dry end of the chenin scale, quite green on the nose and palate but pleasingly balalnced with the grape's trademark richness, and lifted by limey acidity; good assertive food matcher; 13.5% alcohol.

SPAIN

🍷 **8** **Cepa Lebrel Rioja Blanco 2022** £4.99

Dry wine with a grapefruit twang to the green-leafy nose and a suggestion of salinity in the white, fresh fruit; bit of residual sweetness here; 12.5% alcohol.

FORTIFIED WINES

PORTUGAL

🍷 **9** **Armilar 10-Year-Old Tawny Port** £11.99

I'm taking it on trust that Lidl will continue with this Christmas-only special for years to come. It's a nutty-figgy-silky-spicy wood-aged wine of real merit at a decent price for this level, made by proper port house da Silva. Lidl rightly recommend drinking it chilled, as the Portuguese do, as a festive aperitif, but it's a nifty after-dinner wine at room temperature too; 20% alcohol.

SPARKLING WINES

🍷 10 Crémant de Loire Brut £8.99

This is a cracker: joyously foaming and fresh-fruity full-force fizz from deepest south west France. Chenin blanc grapes harmonise white-nut creaminess with refreshing tangy acidity. Delightful sparkler of very evident quality at a keen price; 12% alcohol.

🍷 10 Carpentier Champagne Brut £13.99

I understand this to be Lidl's new house Champagne, replacing Comte de Senneval, which I can now admit I never much liked. This is different: tantalising sweet brioche nose, busy bubbles conveying brisk red-apple fruit and citrus twist, vivid freshness of style, niftily dry but lingering aftertaste; very easy to like and that goes for the price too; 12.5% alcohol.

🍷 9 Montaudon Champagne Brut £14.99

Familiar brand at what seems an anomalous price (at time of writing, this Champagne was priced at £33 on Amazon) but it's definitely the real thing: mellow (not sweet) in colour and style with fine persisting mousse and good fruit-freshness balance; 12% alcohol.

🍷 8 Arestel Cava Brut £5.49

Perkily scented and busily fizzy Catalonian dry sparkler at an unfathomable price; orchard fruit, lemon acidity; 11.5% alcohol. Useful mixer for Bucks Fizz and similar.

Majestic

I couldn't make it to the Majestic tasting this year – unavoidably detained elsewhere – but thank you Majestic for the kind invitation. Instead, I sallied forth to my local Majestic and invested in what I hope is a representative selection at an average of a tenner at mix-six prices. I must say the overall range is impressive – a plethora of New World wines as ever but still very strong on Italy and Spain as well as France, with a particularly good choice of Beaujolais. It's just like the old days.

Majestic has a slick online presence and does home deliveries on an epic scale, but I'm interested to learn that they are back to expanding their high-street presence. A dozen new outlets have opened since the current owners took over in 2019.

There's a new own-label range, 'Chosen by Majestic', of wines up to £10 or so, and I have tried a handful of them, along with items from the longer-established 'Definition' range. And you can now join the Majestic Wine Club which, I quote, "provides members with four cases of wine throughout the year, with each case containing 12-bottles that have been selected by Majestic's expert buyers. Each case reflects a new region or element of winemaking and contains an expertly curated brochure with tasting notes and recipes".

That's the news. And, of course, I should point out that the prices I have given for each wine in the following pages is the 'mix-six' one – typically 20% or so less than the single-bottle rate, in memory of the far-off days when Majestic Wine Warehouses was (or appeared to be) a wholesale-only enterprise.

RED WINES

ARGENTINA

🍷 9 **Bodegas Fabre Alta Yari Gran Corte 2019**   £14.99
I raved about this in last year's edition and it was still on sale as this one was going to press, so do seek it out – especially as the price is down from £16.99 (although the single-bottle-purchase price is still £24.99). Gorgeous, succulent, cabernet franc/malbec blend by incomer from Bordeaux Hervé Joyaux Fabre; 14.5% alcohol.

CHILE

🍷 8 **Mayu Carmenère Appassimento 2019**   £10.99
The Italian winemaking style of including very late-picked grapes to the fermenting blend is used to produce this rich, peppery, raisiny but aboundingly fruity and healthily gripping speciality red (going slightly brown) for meaty occasions and winter comfort; 14.5% alcohol. Reportedly the only appassimento carmenère in the world.

FRANCE

🍷 9 **Château Recougne 2019**   £10.99
Generic Bordeaux Supérieur tasting well above this humble ranking: succulent and rounded cassis fruit with a cedary, smoky slickness; it's mainly merlot but with an unusual addition of carmenère, once a claret standby but now near-extinct in the region; a special wine, generous and drinking very well now; 14.5% alcohol.

🍷 8 **Definition Beaujolais-Villages 2020**   £8.99
Exemplary juicy everyday beaujolais of genuine quality – very good straight from the fridge on the right occasion; 13% alcohol.

🍷 8 **Château Pesquié Terrrasses Ventoux 2020**   £10.99
From one of the Rhône's most distinctive sub-appellations, Ventoux, a darkly savoury food red of spicy distinction; intense, defined garrigue savours; 14% alcohol.

RED WINES

FRANCE

10 Juliénas Les Mouilles Pardon & Fils 2021   £12.99
Outstanding edgy but emphatically ripe classic Beaujolais full of juicy strawberry-cherry brightness with plenty of depth of colour and fruit and very agreeable abrasion – finishes brisk and lively; 13% alcohol. Unusually, the back label advises that this could be 'left in the wine rack for four or five years' and I can believe it. Lovely now, though.

8 Brouilly Château de Pizay 2022   £13.99
Plump, juicily sweet and beguiling classic Brouilly – very good to find Majestic are keeping up their Beaujolais range; very likeable soft, bouncy style, impressively full of red summer fruit savour; 13% alcohol.

ITALY

7 Domodo Negroamaro 2021   £8.99
Light Puglian party red for pizza nights; 12% alcohol.

0 Terredora di Paolo Compagnia Aglianico 2019   £8.99
Reduced on mix-six from an unlikely £14.99, this was awful: lean, passed-over, unworthy. Shame on you, Majestic.

8 Corte Ferro Frappato Nerello Mascalese 2020   £9.99
Effective blend of two indigenous grape varieties from Sicily provides lively brambly fruits, baked earthiness and a good cut of acidity; nicely weighted thoroughly Italian pasta red of character; 13.5% alcohol.

8 De Forville Dolcetto d'Alba 2021   £9.99
An old friend on good form: dark and defined blackberry-pie quite serious Piedmont wine from elusive local grape dolcetto; juicy and complete, finishes very trim; 13% alcohol. An unwelcome innovation since I last tried this, years back, is the horrible polymer 'cork'.

RED WINES

ITALY

🍷 **8** **Dogajolo Carpineto Toscano 2020** **£11.99**
A Majestic speciality since the dawn of time, this attractively packaged (snazzy screwtop) 'super-Tuscan' is really no more than Chianti with a bit of cabernet sauvignon added but it is consistently delicious, rangy, brightly juicy with cherry-raspberry fruit and thoroughly endearing; 13% alcohol.

🍷 **9** **Domini Veneti La Casetta**
     Valpolicella Ripasso Superiore 2019 **£16.99**
Uniquely rich and complex variation on the rightly popular revved-up-Valpolicella genre, this slinky, minty, chocolatey and above all piquantly black-fruity contrivance is of the most delectable weight, texture and balance between opulence and gentle tannic grip, finishing entirely bright; 14% alcohol. A Majestic stalwart that has never faltered.

PORTUGAL

🍷 **8** **Ramos Reserva 2020** **£8.99**
Rich but perkily brambly Alentejo wine with exotic notes of black olive as well as black berries – very savoury and interesting, and with sweet spice and a good grip of ripe tannins; 14.5% alcohol.

ROMANIA

🍷 **9** **Incanta Pinot Noir 2022** **£7.99**
In Romanian *incanta* means 'delight' and this fresh young wine fully lives up to it: plump with proper pinot cherry-raspberry juiciness; 12.5% alcohol. Chills well for warmer days.

RED WINES

SOUTH AFRICA

9 Vergelegen Millrace Cabernet Sauvignon Merlot 2019 £9.99

Vergelegen in Stellenbosch was founded in 1700 and has long produced some of South Africa's grandest wines. Lately, besides the prestige range, this fine institution has moved into the 'everyday' market – and here's one to try. It's a perfectly pitched blend of elegant weight, mineral purity and joyful juiciness; it's ripe (14% alcohol) and sleek, and I'm sure it will age gracefully. And it costs a tenner. Flagship affordable wine from a world-class producer.

8 Chosen by Majestic Rioja Crianza 2020 £8.99

From Majestic's new budget-price own-label range so far of a dozen or so, a young but developed wine with six months of oak-ageing in the *crianza* ('nursery') plump with cassis, mint and warm-spice fruit tasting a lot like Rioja; 13.5% alcohol.

SPAIN

7 La Garnacha Salvaje del Moncayo 2020 £9.99

Gloomy label illustration of what might be a vineyard in Mordor in fact shows the 'wild' garnacha bush vines of Moncayo in the highlands of the Ebro Valley whence this pale middleweight with hedgerow-fruit savours in a wild style all its own; 14.5% alcohol.

9 Bardos Roble Ribera del Duero 2020 £9.99

Cool package – enigmatic figure in a landscape – for this all-tempranillo dark, leafy, liquorice and blackcurrant oaked pungent food wine from prestigious (and pricey) region Ribera del Duero; 14% alcohol.

RED WINES

SPAIN

8 · Definition Rioja Reserva 2018 £12.99

On first opening it was light bordering on lean, failing to chime as a five-year-aged wine of any kind, let alone Rioja. So I put the cork back in. Two days later it was transformed. The air had brought out intensity, a flowering of both fruit and vanilla-oak richness; I'm not making this up. If you do invest in this, decant it well in advance; 13% alcohol.

PINK WINES

ARGENTINA

9 · Alamos Malbec Rosé 2022 £7.99

Stands out. Alluring coppery colour, zingy freshness perhaps owed in part to the 5,000-foot altitude of the vineyards in Mendoza, and assertive sunny fruits evoking rapsberry, plum, even quince; juicy, tangy and 13.5% alcohol. Unusually good value for serious rosé.

FRANCE

8 · Rosé d'Anjou Feu 2021 £5.99

Soft but fresh Loire Valley pink, flush with strawberry ripeness and a lick of rosehip. Old-school rosé with modest 10.5% alcohol at a budget price.

8 · Chosen by Majestic Rosé 2022 £8.99

From Majestic's 2023-launched affordable own-label range, a Pays d'Oc wine clearly inspired by the winning style of neighbouring Provence with rosé; vogueish onion-skin colour, fruit-blossom aromas, crisp texture to the delicate redcurrant-alpine strawberry fruit, lemon lift and definitely dry; 12.5% alcohol.

PINK WINES

🍷 8 Côtes des Roses Rosé 2022 £10.99

FRANCE

It comes in an elaborate bottle, the base embossed with a pattern of roses so you could push it into the sand at your seaside picnic and leave a floral imprint. And this isn't even the principal attraction. It's made by prolific grower-merchant Gerard Bertrand under the broad Languedoc appellation but is easily comparable to grander Côtes de Provence pinks; fine coppery colour, redcurrant, raspberry and grapefruit scents and a welcome crispness of style to the summery fruits; 13% alcohol. It grows on you.

🍷 8 AIX Coteaux d'Aix en Provence Rosé 2022 £22.99

Majestic have been doing this magnificent magnum for ever – and certainly from long before the current rosé craze kicked off. And it's as good as ever: fine sunset colour, tempting whiff of strawberry and citrus, generously ripe corresponding fruit embracing white peach, and, it says in my note, 15% alcohol. Can this be right? Standard 75cl bottles don't seem to be listed, but you can go the other way and pick up a double magnum for £64.99, if you have the strength.

🍷 8 Pasqua 11 Minutes Rosé 2022 £12.99

ITALY

Worthy successor to last year's excellent vintage this Veronese oddity from Syrah grapes has a healthy flesh-pink colour and exuberant fruit-blossom nose translating into plump savours with freshness and a twang of lime-grapefruit acidity; 12.5% alcohol. The 11 minutes alluded to comprise the time the black-skinned grapes were left in contact with the new-pressed juice before run-off – imparting the delicate colour in the approved manner.

WHITE WINES

9 **Shaw & Smith M3 Chardonnay 2022**   **£29.99**
Aussie chardonnay at its peak – and arguably at a fraction of
the price of the kind of white burgundy with which I assume
it aspires to compete. It's pure gold in colour, shot with green,
rich in sweet-apple and white peach succulent fruit, mineral in
its poised purity and plush all the way to the textbook brisk
acidity; 13.5% alcohol. Special-occasion wine.

8 **Chosen by Majestic Muscadet 2022**   **£8.99**
Likeable spin on the Loire-estuary bone-dry moules-matcher
theme. Tastes riper than most, with red rather sour apple fruit
and more contemplative in length; 11.5% alcohol. Good augur
for Majestic's new modestly priced own-label range.

9 **Mâcon-Villages Caves de Lugny**
Les Pierres Blanches 2021   **£9.99**
Yardstick dry white burgundy with inimitable Mâconnais
minerality, crisp-pear-lemon juiciness and a lick of leesiness (no
oak) all in fine balance; 13% alcohol. Extravagantly reduced
from single-bottle price of £14.99.

8 **Definition Sauternes 2014 37.5cl**   **£10.99**
Sumptuous maturing dessert wine of ambrosial lusciousness
definingly balanced by clean acidity, gold in colour and
richness. It is reportedly made by a classed growth estate of
the Sauternes, and 2014 happens to be an outstanding vintage;
13% alcohol.

8 **Definition Mâcon-Villages 2021**   **£11.99**
Rich green-tinged colour and the familiar vegetal/brassica
Mâconnais chardonnay bloom lead into a fine mineral ripe-
apple delicately peachy fruit, racy and lush; 13% alcohol.

WHITE WINES

FRANCE

Y 8 Louis Violland Mercurey Blanc 2019　　　£19.99

Lush successor to last year's 2018 which I praised at the wrong price, a fine Chalonnais (Burgundy outlier) plump with peach and sweet-apple chardonnay savour, controlled oak creaminess and lifting citrus; 14% alcohol.

GERMANY

Y 9 Dr Loosen Slate Hill Riesling 2022　　　£9.99

Trace of spritz in this delectably racy moselle – citrus zing in wondrous harmony with the lavish grapey-green-apple fruit, vivaciously fresh and stimulating; 8.5% alcohol. Ernst Loosen makes world-class generic rieslings at remarkably reasonable prices – a name to look out for.

ITALY

Y 7 Inama Soave Classico 2022　　　£14.99

Pleasant, fresh, green-apple, very dry rendering of famous Verona wine; a bit ordinary for the money, I thought; 12% alcohol.

Y 8 Feudi di San Gregorio Greco di Tufo 2022　　　£14.99

Fine new vintage of this exotic dry wine from the Campania region, neighbour to Naples. Aromas of conference pear, blanched almond and lemon zest coalesce in the fruit into a complex and stimulating whole with a natural richness partially down to the eight months the wine spent on its lees before bottling; 13% alcohol.

NEW ZEALAND

Y 9 Definition Sauvignon Blanc 2022　　　£8.49

Majestic has prevailed upon Brent Maris, the maestro behind cult Marlborough brand The Ned, to come up with this remarkable all-sauvignon blend from the region: big-flavoured grassy-lush green-fruit classic Kiwi flavours with tropical hints and lemon twang; 13% alcohol. It's special, and well-priced.

WHITE WINES

NEW ZEALAND

8 The Ned Pinot Grigio 2022 £9.99

Aromatic wine nothing like the rubbish that passes for PG in northern Italy, this has a distinct blush to its colour imparted by brief steeping of the pink-skinned fruit and a delicately smoky savour to the orchard and more exotic fruit evocations; dry, fresh and a versatile food match; 14% alcohol.

PORTUGAL

9 Adega de Pegões Selected Harvest White 2021 £9.99

Remarkably plausible white-burgundy-style dry Setubal wine from a mix of native grapes with a glug of chardonnay. It's party fermented and mostly matured in oak casks and tastes like it – supple, white-nut-rich but with a note of crisp-apple freshness; 13% alcohol.

SPAIN

9 The Guv'nor Vino Blanco £7.99

Off-the-wall blend of verdejo, sauvignon blanc and oaked chardonnay from unstated regional origins and more than one vintage; grassy but lush, plump with sunny orchard-fruit ripeness, and pricked with lime; 12.5% alcohol.

Marks & Spencer

It's been a good year for M&S overall and a vintage one for M&S wines. I cannot recall a time when the range on offer has been as inspired as it is now. And what's more, the wines are better value, in context, than ever before.

Virtually all the wines are as always M&S own-brand. It's the distinct ranges that are new, starting with the wondrous 'Found' wines from what might be called unexpected or out-of-the-way places like Georgia and Romania as well obscure corners of Italy or Iberia. And there are economy wines at what M&S drinks boss Andrew Shaw calls "extremely affordable" prices, starting at £5.50 – including several highly commended here this year.

Next up are M&S Classics, the range launched, as I recall, mid-Covid, and now extending to more than 30 wines including, natch, Beaujolais, Picpoul de Pinet, Vinho Verde and Vouvray – all included here.

Latest addition is the M&S Collection. Smartly attired posh wines that I discovered at the 2023 M&S summer tasting, are as good as they look. Highlights include an exceptional Mendoza malbec and an unusually sensibly priced St Emilion along with my Rioja Gran Reserva of the year.

I could go on but I should add instead that in my experience the choice of wines in the stores can be very variable. It's worth looking online, where the whole list is on offer (by six-bottle case) and there are always a good number on promo price. And of course, all the wines, along with other M&S groceries, are available too on Ocado at what seem to be the same prices you'd pay in store or online at M&S itself.

RED WINES

ARGENTINA

9 M&S Collection Tradición Malbec 2022   £12.00
From M&S's smartly labelled premium range, a darkly maroon Mendoza pure varietal with potent, peppery savours to the rich black fruit; easy weight, finishing grippy and 14.5% alcohol.

AUSTRALIA

**8 Coonawarra Cabernet Sauvignon
Special Reserve 2021**   £10.00
Blood red colour, warm cassis whiffs and ripe cabernet fruit, intense and very easy to like; 14.5% alcohol.

8 Lock Keeper's Reserve Shiraz 2022   £10.00
This stood out as rather restrained in the context of 'upfront' Aussie shiraz; comfortably cushiony baked black fruits in wholesome balance; works well; 13.5% alcohol. I have seen this reasonably priced wine on offer at as much as a third off.

**8 M&S Collection Ebenezer & Seppeltsfield
Barossa Valley Shiraz 2021**   £14.00
Standout wine that matches Aussie upfront fruitiness to Rhône-like poise and purity to make an ideally weighted and rewarding food red for special occasions; 14.5% alcohol.

AUSTRIA

8 M&S Found Zweigelt 2021   £8.50
Zweigelt is a grape created by Austrian botanist Friedrich Zweigelt in 1922 and it has long since been the nation's premier indigenous variety – there's immortality for you. The wine is a beautiful colour and has an intense core flavour evoking raspberries, cherries and bramble, finishing brisk and clean; 13% alcohol.

RED WINES

CHILE

🍷 **8** **M&S Ya'Po Merlot 2021** £6.50

Plenty of black-cherry charm in this juicy party red; a nice stalky spine in the fruit gives it freshness and shape; 13.5% alcohol.

FRANCE

🍷 **8** **M&S Fitou 2021** £7.50

Quite refined for a Fitou – an AC of Languedoc known for big spicy flavours and sometimes hardness – this does have a warming garrigue ripeness to the sunny black-fruit savours dusted delicately with pepperiness and a finely judged weight; good brisk acidity; 13.5% alcohol. It grows on you.

🍷 **9** **M&S Classics No. 25 Beaujolais Villages 2022** £10.00

M&S always seems to me to have charged high prices for its Beaujolais but I don't begrudge them this one – a jolly, vigorous, new wine with juicy blue-tinged fruit and lasting summer-fruit savours; 13% alcohol. Try it cool on warmer days.

🍷 **8** **M&S Fleurie 2022** £12.00

Substantial Beaujolais from one of the region's elite *crus*; bouncy and still quite grippy with tannin; 13% alcohol.

🍷 **9** **M&S Collection Saint-Emilion 2019** £16.00

Particularly delicious Bordeaux wine by right-bank legend Christian Moueix of Château Pétrus, this generic merlot-led blend expresses, dare I say it, the true St Emilion style: silky but unoaked with elegant ripeness, evident structure and the mysterious minerality of the famous appellation; really lovely claret from a good vintage to drink now, not to keep; 14% alcohol.

RED WINES

FRANCE

🍷 8 M&S Collection Margaux 2020 £22.00

Immediately likeable young claret from the revered appellation of Margaux is from Château Dauzac, one of the élite estates ranked *Grand Cru Classé* in the 1855 classification of the top wines of Bordeaux. Dauzac is a very fine producer to this day, and the 2020 vintage of the *grand vin* itself costs about £50. Try this as an intro: it's already supple and lush and will develop in bottle for years; 13.5% alcohol.

GEORGIA

🍷 8 M&S Found Saperavi 2021 £9.00

Saperavi is the national grape of Georgia, native to the Caucasus and one of the few *teinturier* varieties – wine grapes with coloured rather than clear juice. In this all-saperavi red you get an inky colour, bold, even pungent, brambly nose and wholesome fruit compote savours with a kind of apple-crumble-topping richness; beguiling wine, easy to like; 13% alcohol.

ITALY

🍷 9 Rustica Sicilian Red 2022 £6.00

New-squished redcurrant is evident amid the ripe and healthy flavours of this very pleasant sticky-pasta matcher from inspired Sicilian co-op Settesoli; finishes brisk and dry; 12% alcohol. It reminds me of that long-gone M&S Sicilian delight, Popolino Rosso.

🍷 9 Governo all'uso Toscano 2019 £9.00

Governo is a technique with very late-picked grapes that have dried on the vines. The concentrated must is added to fermented wine to add colour, weight and general interest. This one, mainly sangiovese, the Chianti grape, has been treated with 1 to 10 ratio of governo from cabernet sauvignon grapes. It's great: dark and gutsy with wild berry fruits and a proper nutskin dry finish; 14% alcohol.

RED WINES

9 **La Cascata Passivento 2021** £10.00

Robust Puglian blend of negroamaro with primitivo includes fruit dried to boost juice concentration – as evidenced by the succulent, spicy intensity of this delicious winter warmer; 14% alcohol. M&S have been known to offer this at a one-third discount.

9 **Notte Rossa Primitivo di Manduria 2020** £12.00

This smartly packaged Puglian heavyweight is near-raisiny in its dark concentration but contrives to be juicy and lipsmacking in the glass; bursting with spicy black fruits, rich from oak contact and finishing perfectly clean; 14% alcohol.

8 **Pontenari Toscana Rosso 2020** £12.00

Blend of two-thirds sangiovese, the Chianti grape, with one of cabernet and merlot making a swish, rounded cassis-sour-cherry-raspberry combo of rich concentration capped by a proper nutskin-dry finish; 14% alcohol.

8 **M&S Collection Poggio Tosco Chianti
Classico Riserva 2019** £16.00

Top-drawer Chianti from a grand estate, Villa Poggio Salvi, is riserva, so aged in oak a while, but still likeably vigorous with red fruits and violet aromas in the proper Chianti way, and it has a mellow maturity besides; 13.5% alcohol.

8 **M&S Collection Pieronte Barolo 2019** £18.00

I'm not much of a fan of Barolo, Italy's most vaunted red wine, finding the brands you get in supermarkets tending to the thin, spirity and stewed. But here's a good one, with jewel-like garnet colour, attractive rose-petal perfume and a decent heft of sharp-cherry, slickly ripe fruit, maturing but not yet drying out; 14% alcohol.

RED WINES

NEW ZEALAND

8 **Clocktower Pinot Noir 2021** £14.00

Swishy Marlborough pinot by famed Wither Hills winery; full and firm in juicy red summer fruits with elegant silkiness and firm grip; 13.5% alcohol. It's a more forward wine than, say, a comparable good-quality generic burgundy would be, but it might well give more pleasure – and value.

PORTUGAL

9 **M&S Found Alicante Bouschet 2021** £8.00

A fetching old photo of a tram, presumably in Lisbon, graces the label of this impactful ripe-cassis and red-berry Alentejo wine of middling weight trimmed with sweet tannins; 14% alcohol.

8 **Lisboa Bonita 2021** £10.00

This dark-fruit-packed Lisbon wine adds mint and spice to the weighty black-fruit flavours giving it an almost porty heft; substantial and satisfying, with ripe tannins to trim; 13.5% alcohol.

8 **Quinta de Fafide Reserva 2020** £11.00

Intense and conspicuously oak-matured table wine from Port country that leaves no doubt of its Douro Valley origin and beguiles with minty-slinky succulence to the dark berry fruit; 14% alcohol.

SOUTH AFRICA

8 **Daniel's Drift Merlot Fairtrade 2022** £6.00

I was going to say plausible, but pleasurable is fairer, of this mellow merlot's sweetly ripe cherry-berry dark fruits, convincingly complete and in balance; 14% alcohol.

RED WINES

SOUTH AFRICA

🍷 8 **Houdamond Pinotage 2018** £15.00
Deep crimson colour, powerful cassis scent and a relishable tarry note to the intense black fruit mark out this premium pinotage – the Cape's own indigenous grape; 14% alcohol. Fans should try this.

SPAIN

🍷 8 **M&S This is Spanish Red 2021** £5.50
All-tempranillo, juicy, blackcurranty, healthy party red is complete in its structure and nicely balanced; 13.5% alcohol.

🍷 8 **El Duque de Miralta Ribera del Duero 2019** £12.00
The ritzy oaked pure tempranillo lives up to expectations of the grand Ribera del Duero, very dark, silky and minty-spicy black-fruit flavours wrapped up in firm but friendly tannins; 14% alcohol. This will develop in bottle if you give it half a chance.

🍷 10 **M&S Collection El Duque de Miralta Rioja
Gran Reserva 2016** £16.00
Perfect. My Rioja of the year. Succulent blackcurrant perfume with creamy oak halo and lush, balanced, silky, dark, dark fruit to match. The weight and texture are sublime with just the right genteel decay from long cask and bottle ageing; 14%. I'd drink it soon. The price is completely fair.

PINK WINES

FRANCE

🍷 8 **St Mont Fleur De Lise 2022** £8.00
Vanishingly pale pink colour but brightly fruity dry rosé of clear quality, made by Producteurs Plaimont, the excellent leading wine co-operative of Pyrenean south west France; 12% alcohol.

PINK WINES

🍷 8 Quintessence Méditerranée Rosé 2022   £9.50
Fancy package largely from merlot grapes grown in the Vaucluse (around Avignon); cheery, salmon-coloured, strawberry- and lemon-perfumed dry refresher with abundant summer fruit savours; 12% alcohol.

🍷 8 Myrtia Moschofilero Assyrtiko Dry Rosé 2022 £10.00
It is dry, just as the name on the label asserts, and it's brightly crisp as well, lifting the delicate fruit – I've written blood orange in my note – to a level of interest that warrants the price; 12.5% alcohol.

🍷 9 Familia Castaño Yecla Organic Rosé 2021   £7.50
Shell pink, softly plump, strawberry-suggestive food wine from Mediterranean enclave of Yecla where the constituent black-skinned monastrell grape prospers. This is a convincing dry rosé with plenty of fruit and a proper acidity; 12.5% alcohol.

WHITE WINES

🍷 8 Burra Brook Sauvignon Blanc 2021   £7.00
Perennial party white with gooseberry-grassy aromas and corresponding crisply fresh green fruits with lemon lift; likeably light in body and woof at just 10.5% alcohol. If the 2022 vintage has arrived, it should be an equally safe bet.

🍷 8 Lock Keeper's Reserve Chardonnay 2022   £10.00
Reassuringly generous and sunny oaked full-fruit chardonnay including a small measure of semillon that might be contributing the pineapple and mango notes I believe I detected; big flavours nicely balanced; 13% alcohol.

WHITE WINES

CHILE

8 **Ya'Po Sauvignon Blanc 2022** £6.50

Liked this new wine from the 2021 vintage last year, so pleased to find the next one just as perky with gooseberry-grassy aromas, lushness and characteristic Chilean ripeness; 12.5% alcohol.

8 **M&S Classics No. 15 Picpoul de Pinet 2022** £9.00

Crisp, saline, fresh and full rendering of the understandably popular Picpoul style from the sun-baked vineyards of blissful Montagnac at the crossroads of the Mediterranean with the Cevennes; 12.5% alcohol.

8 **M&S Classics No 33 Vouvray 2022** £9.00

Lovely balanced Loire Valley classic chenin blanc tending to the *moelleux* style of Vouvray's sweeter wines, but I'd still call this a dry wine to enjoy with shellfish, charcuterie or salads. It's honeyed but brightly lit with white fruits; 12% alcohol.

FRANCE

9 **M&S Collection Chablis 2020** £15.00

Fine gunflint-aroma to this full-on wine – good intensity of mineral chardonnay fruit but still edgy and tangy in the Chablis tradition, and I believe benefiting from time in bottle; 12.5% alcohol.

8 **M&S Collection Pouilly-Fumé La Tuilerie 2021** £15.00

Textbook gooseberry-asparagus-seagrass sauvignon blanc from Pouilly-sur-Loire, near neighbour to Sancerre (see next wine); full of green-fruit savour and stimulating freshness; 12.5% alcohol.

WHITE WINES

FRANCE

8 **M&S Collection Sancerre Les Ruettes 2020** £16.00
Authentic river-fresh pure sauvignon blanc from the Loire's grandest appellation that's glitteringly good and flinty-mineral even though from a comparatively mature vintage; 13% alcohol.

10 **Les Domaines Brocard Organic Chablis 2021** £17.00
Jean-Marc Brocard is famed for the lushness of his Chablis, all of which has been organically produced for the last 25 years. This one conforms: fine gold colour, piquant struck-match aroma, complex sweet-and-tart apple-flesh fruits, very mineral, lemony finish, feels extravagant and expensive; 12.5% alcohol.

GEORGIA

8 **M&S Found Mtsvane 2022** £9.00
Mtsvane (pronounced mahts-vah-neh and meaning green, fresh or new) is a green-skinned Georgian grape variety that deserves more attention. This new addition to M&S's 'Found' range has a delightful meadow-flower aroma, an instant tang of crisp freshness on the tongue and a fine mélange of white fruit flavours piqued with sherbet and lemon; 13.5% alcohol. A distinctive dry aperitif wine from a brave nation.

8 **M&S Tbilvino Qvevris 2021** £9.00
Yup, Georgia specialises in impenetrable wine names. But this one is not of the grape, rkatsiteli (you work it out) but of the Tbilvino winery, where some of the wines are matured on their skins in *qvevri*, huge clay jars buried in the earth. It's a vinification method dating back a long way, in a region that's been making wine for maybe 8,000 years. So now you know. Do try the wine. It's gold in hue, almost fino-sherry-like in its heft and intriguingly plush, full of fresh-fruit savours, quite dry and, I'll venture, a great partner for shellfish.

WHITE WINES

GERMANY

🍷 9 **M&S Found Weissburgunder 2021** £9.50

This is pinot blanc from the Rhine, much in the way they do it in neighbouring Alsace but with extra raciness to the lush vegetal herbaceous brassica-orchard-fruit capped with tangy citrus acidity; lovely all-purpose dry white of real distinction; 12.5% alcohol.

HUNGARY

🍷 8 **M&S Found Furmint 2021** £8.00

This dry, aromatic wine from Hungary's Tokaj region is a welcome nod by M&S to vinous diversity. Made from the furmint grape, famous as the constituent of ultra-sweet Tokaj 'dessert' wines, this is a daisy-fresh crisp apple-pear party white with an elusive petillance and a little lick of richness ahead of the tangy finish; 12.5% alcohol. Made by serious Tokaj estate Chateau Dereszla.

ITALY

🍷 8 **M&S Rustica Bianca 2022** £6.00

A simple Sicilian dry white with nuance – crispness, fleeting salinity, basket of white-flesh fruit flavours, tangy edge; Italian, you might call it; 12% alcohol.

🍷 8 **La Prendina Estate Pinot Grigio 2022** £10.00

Of numerous PGs tried at M&S I liked this old friend the best: almost sweetly ripe and leesy with a trace of smokiness – and perfectly dry and trim at the edge; natural-tasting food matcher from the Lombardy region; 12.5% alcohol.

🍷 8 **M&S Collection Gavi del Commune di Gavi 2022** £13.00

Made by Piedmont's giant producer Araldica this turns out to hail from a vineyard of just a dozen acres. It is accordingly select in style: fine colour, keen lemony-vegetal nose and lush mineral savours, 12.5% alcohol. Clearly a special wine – a treat for Gavi aficionados.

WHITE WINES

PORTUGAL

8 **M&S Classics Vinho Verde 2022** £8.00
Enduring quirky dry 'green wine' from the Minho Valley so known because the grapes are picked early on. It has the right gentle spritz and crisp-lemony savours, very dry except for the residual sugar favoured for export styles; just 10% alcohol.

ROMANIA

8 **M&S Found Feteasca Regala 2022** £7.00
Feteasca regala is Romania's indigenous grape, and the flagship variety for the country's fast-developing wine industry. This aromatic off-dry but refreshing aperitif wine has pleasing notes of peach and baked pear (clove included); 12.5% alcohol. From Transylvanian winery Cramele Recas, where the winemakers hail respectively from Australia and Spain.

10 **M&S This Is Chardonnay 2022** £6.20
Lush Cape pure-varietal dry party wine; brimming with ripe red-apple fruit, leesy natural richness and briskness of tangy acidity; 13% alcohol. For this money, as good as it gets, and a proper coup for M&S's enterprising budget ranges.

SOUTH AFRICA

8 **M&S Vibrant & Zesty 2022** £5.50
It's all sauvignon blanc, in the fuller Cape style with an agreeable abrasion to the green fruit; 12.5% alcohol.

8 **Daniel's Drift Fairtrade Sauvignon Blanc 2022** £6.00
Asparagus note and lots of interest through the fresh green but sweetly ripe fruit and lifting citrus edge; 12.5% alcohol.

8 **Ken Forrester Stellenbosch Reserve
Chenin Blanc 2020** £12.00
Lavish gold colour but really rather a restrained rendering of the Cape chenin blanc style: fleeting honeysuckle on the nose, juicy white orchard fruits lifted by citrus, all in elegant balance; 13.5% alcohol. Grown-up dry wine, clearly very well made.

WHITE WINES

SOUTH AFRICA

🍷 8 **M&S Stellenrust Wild Ferment Chardonnay 2022** £12.00

Fairtrade wine has the additional virtue of wild-yeast fermentation – rare in these times of cultured yeasts – and it does somehow have the glow of a naturally made product. It's lush, pure and long-flavoured, bright, mineral and chardonnay all the way; 13% alcohol.

FORTIFIED WINES

SPAIN

🍷 9 **M&S Manzanilla Sherry** £8.00

Tangy seaside-fresh bone-dry very pale style from excellent Bodegas Williams & Humbert; quite delicious and jolly good value; 15% alcohol. Serve chilled to icy in a small wine glass, not a thimble.

SPARKLING WINES

ENGLAND

🍷 9 **Bramble Hill Sparkling Brut** £16.00

Introduced just a year ago by M&S, this Kentish fizz is brisk in crunchy orchard fruits warmed with bakery notes and lifted by citrus tang, and it's brisk, too, in its eager persistent bubbliness. And here's the thing: it's made not by the second-fermentation-in-bottle method of Champagne, but in the second-fermentation-in-a-great-big-tank method – as is prosecco. But it's nothing like prosecco. As well as being lastingly sparkling (prosecco droops pronto) it's made from the Champagne grape varieties, and it's made brilliantly; in this case from the harvest of 2021; 12.5% alcohol. The price is modest for top-quality English sparkling wine, and I hope other UK wineries might be inspired to follow suit.

SPARKLING WINES

⚲ 9 Champagne Delacourt Brut £23.00

I'm liking M&S's non-vintage house Champagne better and better. It's mellow in style – the base wines date back to 2016 – with juicy red-apple savours and biscuity notes to the notably tiny-bubble mousse; 12.5% alcohol. The Delacourt range was launched in 2018 with this one at £30; the prices have gradually eased so the wines now compete for value with the formidable competition from the likes of Sainsbury and Tesco. I love a Champagne war.

⚲ 9 Champagne Delacourt Medium Dry £25.00

It's Champagne for those who don't like their fizz too 'green' in the brut style (invented 150 years ago for the British market) but that doesn't mean it's sweet. Mellow's the word, and it's gorgeous; 12.5% alcohol.

⚲ 8 Champagne Delacourt Rosé Brut £25.00

Certainly one of the pink Champagnes I've liked best this year at any price. This combines pleasing colour with mellow fruits that actually taste pink in the way of summer strawberries and the like and very fresh and lively into the bargain; 12.5% alcohol.

⚲ 9 M&S Cava Brut £7.50

Made for M&S by Catalan giant Freixenet (pronounced frej-nay) this is fully-fledged fizz made by the same method as Champagne, with its own frisky crisp-fruit savours, delicious and refreshing; 11.5% alcohol. The price speaks for itself.

FRANCE

SPAIN

Morrisons

I've been fretting that this redoubtable retailer must be ailing under the mantle of its new owner, American private-equity monster CD&R. I heard that the cost of the £6.6 billion borrowed to buy Morrisons out is now so vast that the supermarkets' total profits are insufficient even to cover the interest payments.

But there have been reassuring words from David Potts, Morrisons' seasoned CEO, who told *The Times* he was confident private-equity ownership would be good news in the long run: "when CD&R eventually exit this business, it will be in a better place than when they arrived – I've absolutely no doubt about that at all".

So that's all good then. And now I have been to a big Morrisons tasting for the first time in years, the news is even more encouraging. The wine department is in good heart. Diversity, quality and interest are rife. And value is holding up very well indeed.

It's hard to pin down, but I have always found Morrisons in-store wine shelves bewildering. Maybe they're cramming a big choice into too-small a space. Or maybe it's the bunting: price offers of ever-changing complexity are a perpetual presence. But it's worth paying heed. The wines are well-chosen, the shelf prices sensible and the discounts frequently generous, including regular 25%-off everything for purchases of x numbers of bottles, any mix. Specific offers on the excellent 'The Best' own-label wines are a frequent feature.

Highlights this year include several from that range, including the 2021 Single Vineyard Chilean Pinot Noir, the 2020 Premier Cru Chablis, and the lovely Palo Cortado sherry at a risible £6.50 per 375ml. Morrisons' own sherry range is a wonder in itself.

RED WINES

9 **The Best Gran Montana Uco Valley Malbec 2020** £11.00
The deep intense purple colour suggests it might taste raw but this is round and developed with blackberry-blueberry juiciness and a friendly grip at the finish in the best malbec tradition; brief oak ageing works well; 14% alcohol.

8 **Vinalba Patagonia Malbec 2021** £11.00
The difference is that it's not from Argentina's Andean region of Mendoza but from Patagonia, most of which is a plateau of steppe or desert. Nice luxury wine though, dark and gently spiced, easy weight and oak-caressed; 14.5% alcohol.

8 **Trivento Golden Reserve Malbec 2020** £17.00
Big-brand wine adorned with medals and it doesn't disappoint. It's plush with long spicy black-fruit flavours in fine balance with an authentic new-leather whiff and firm but friendly finish; 13.5% alcohol.

8 **The Best Barossa Valley Shiraz 2021** £11.00
On tasting day I liked this easily the best of the Aussie reds I tried: eager whack of upfront, darkly baked, gently spiced fruit of ideal weight, finishing brisk and clean; savoury and comforting; 13.9% alcohol.

8 **The Best Chilean Merlot 2022** £8.25
Packs in a lot of firm black-cherry fruit in the approved merlot manner, but wholesomely balanced and lipsmacking; 13.5% alcohol.

8 **The Best Chilean Pinot Noir 2022** £9.25
Chunky Casablanca wine with minerality as well as weight, a full-fruit pinot in the earthy Chilean style; 13.5% alcohol.

ARGENTINA

AUSTRALIA

CHILE

RED WINES

CHILE

8 The Best Single Vineyard Pinot Noir 2021 £11.50
Pale but impactful wine by dependable Vina Errazuriz; generous ripeness of summer red soft fruits and a deluxe silkiness (it's oak matured); plump in the Chilean manner but with an elegance evoking the burgundy tradition; 14% alcohol.

8 Chevaliers St Martin Bordeaux 2021 £6.00
Cheap claret's not always a delight, but this purple merlot-based generic has brambly charms and wholesome balance; 12.5% alcohol.

9 Calvet Carcassonne 2022 £7.50
This generic Languedoc Carignan/Caradoc blend under huge Calvet brand is arrestingly good: dark berry flavours enriched with bitter chocolate and sour cherry highlights make for an artfully poised food red (meat, cassoulet, winter warmers) finishing bright, savoury and satisfying; 14% alcohol.

FRANCE

8 Château Mauriac 2019 £8.25
Good-looking package that makes an immediate impression with its plummy-blackcurranty perfume and matching rounded healthily hefty fruit; very pleasant surprise at this price for a Bordeaux wine; 13% alcohol.

8 The Best Cahors Malbec 2020 £9.00
Nice dense jewel-like ruby colour to this oak-matured Cahors made with 15% merlot, which might explain the agreeable sweetness partnering the charcoal and black-fruit robustness of this generous, grippy food wine (barbecue included); 13% alcohol.

RED WINES

FRANCE

8 **The Best Languedoc Red 2022** £8.50
Syrah-led blend with wholesome hedgerow-fruit aromas and flavours in abundance, edged with a friendly clench of ripe tannins; 13% alcohol.

9 **Paul Mas Réserve Pinot Noir 2021** £9.50
Mediterranean rendition of the great grape of Burgundy honouring the cherry-raspberry perkiness of the style and adding welcome weight and intensity to the fruit; I really liked this substantial and relishable food red (poultry and game come to mind) which you could call New World in style, but has olde worlde elegance and definition; 13% alcohol.

9 **La Quaintrelle Lesquerde 2021** £10.00
Quaintly named syrah-grenache-carignan hailing from the remote hill village of Lesquerde in the Côtes du Roussillon, the sunniest spot in France (325 days a year). The dark, structured and substantial black fruits tell the story, with spikes of peppery fruits-of-the-forest savour; 13% alcohol. Fascinating, delightful food wine (grilled meat, loud cheeses, you name it) in an impressive package.

9 **Juliénas Georges Duboeuf 2019** £15.00
Purply young juicy bouncing Beaujolais cru of shining quality and thoroughly stimulating character; 14% alcohol. As good as Beaujolais gets and I got this for eight quid on promo. Juliénas isn't the best-known of the 10 crus but it certainly ranks with the best, and at relatively sensible prices.

RED WINES

FRANCE

🍷 **8** **Bonpas Vacqueyras 2020** £16.00
Vacqueyras is among the elite village appellations of the Côtes du Rhône and the wines have become very expensive. This one, believe it or not, is a bit of a bargain: dark, weighty and slick with creamy, spicy, minty black-fruit savours all in balance with juicy tannins; 14% alcohol.

🍷 **10** **Villa Verde Montepulciano d'Abruzzo 2022** £6.00
Dense, blood-red colour, plum and sour-cherry nose, lovely juicy, bouncingly delicious, remarkably well-knit and balanced classic wine of its kind from Italy's picturesque east midlands with true verve, all at a ridiculously low price; 13% alcohol.

ITALY

🍷 **8** **Piccini Memoro** £8.50
My bottle had a Gold sticker from Decanter's 2019 wines of the year judging, which might seem a shade out of date, but this is a non-vintage wine, made from grapes of more than one year. From an old Tuscan outfit still in family ownership, it's a big plump blend with a bit of cushiony appassimento from grapes – including primitivo, montepulciano and even merlot – brought in from several Italian regions; warmly spicy black-cherry fruit nicely trimmed with acidity; 14% alcohol. Widely sold across the supermarkets and widely discounted, too.

🍷 **9** **The Best Negroamaro 2021** £9.00
A fine ruby colour to this excellent Puglian pure varietal leads on to generous, grilled black berry fruits and a likeable liquorice savour. Comforting winter red with a tight nutskin finish – a good match for sticky pasta and risotto; 13.5% alcohol. A bottle I reopened on day two had benefited from 'breathing', so worth decanting.

RED WINES

ITALY

8 The Best Organic Montepulciano
d'Abruzzo 2021 £8.50
Juicy summer red with good berry intensity and bright fruit
flavours – a fine example of the regional style but for value not a
patch on the top-scoring Villa Verde wine above; 13% alcohol.

8 Colpasso Appassimento 2021 £10.00
Likeable Sicilian wine, zanily labelled, from the native nero
d'avola grape and made with a proportion of concentrated
must (a technique first devised for Valpolicella up north in
Verona) to produce an extra-ripe, pleasingly abrading effect,
enhanced by oak maturation; 14% alcohol.

8 The Best Valpolicella Ripasso 2018 £11.50
Gently weighty sweet-dry confection from Verona, artfully
balanced to match winter feasts; black-cherry ripeness, coffee-
chocolate notes; brisk finish; 13.5% alcohol.

8 Nipozzano Chianti Rufina Riserva 2019 £16.00
Grand Tuscan red from the noble Frescobaldi family. Decent
mature Chianti with a bit of pedigree – wine from the Castello
Nipozzano was a favourite of our own King Henry VIII.
Slinky, dark and substantial, it's a dependable special-occasion
standby; 13.5% alcohol. I paid £12 on multibuy.

8 The Best Amarone 2020 £17.00
Amarone translates, oddly enough, as 'bitter' in this case
referring to the empyrumatic (burnt) character of this style of
wine, made with the addition of heat-dried grape must to the
base wine, Valpolicella. In this one from the Cantine di Soave,
the co-op behind Morrison's excellent white Soave wines, the
flavours strongly evoke coffee and fierce cocoa, creating intense
dark flavours that are rich, rather than sweet; 14.5% alcohol.
Good of its kind.

RED WINES

ITALY

8 **The Best Barolo 2018** £19.00

Made by Araldica, a major co-operative of 140 growers in Piedmont, this isn't your 'grand cru' kind of Barolo but it's not bad: pale, rusty colour, limpid, mouth-puckering minty-cherry rather spirity fruit and a certain earthy seductiveness finishing sweet but with a very dry edge; 14% alcohol. Yup, that's Barolo. If you like what is commonly called Italy's premier wine, try this one as it's (most unusually) under twenty quid.

NEW ZEALAND

8 **Villa Maria Private Bin Pinot Noir 2020** £13.00

Benchmark Kiwi pinot, pale and interesting with an alluring cherry-strawberry perfume, a palpable purity and poise on the palate and a welcome plumpness afforded by oak-cask maturing of part of the blend; a class act on good form in this vintage; 13.5% alcohol.

PORTUGAL

8 **Cidade Branca 2021** £8.75

Grippy, leafy and stalky – all in a good way – full-bodied bramble-plum Alentejo wine that stands out from the crowd as a particular kind of food-matcher. It will flatter exotic menus from grilled sardines to richly sauced meat dishes and salty bacon treats; 14% alcohol. Cidade Branca means 'white city' referring to Estremoz at the northern tip of the Alentejo region east of Lisbon, where the main business has long been marble quarrying, but is now cutting out a name for itself in winemaking. Nice buy especially at the £5.25 I paid on promo.

8 **Porta 6 2021** £8.50

From Lisboa, the vine-growing region closest to the Portuguese capital, a robust party red made from the grapes that go into Port – as you might guess from the sweet-spicy-spirity aroma and warming heft of fruit; 13.5% alcohol.

RED WINES

SPAIN

5 **Montelciego Rioja Reserva 2016** £9.00
I paid £5.62 on multibuy but regretted it even at that price.
Dull and untypical.

9 **Pata Negra Toro 2019** £8.00
Named after Spain's famous black-footed Iberico pig, a
deep-purple, densely mouthfilling and ripely savoury pure
tempranillo with tell-tale blackberry fruit and creamy slickness;
a very pleasant surprise from the emerging Toro region of
Spain's northwest; 14.5% alcohol.

8 **The Best Marques de los**
Rios Rioja Crianza 2019 £8.50
By Bodega Muriel, the blackcurrant fruit in this crianza (one
year in cask) is in healthy balance with the oak, and might
develop; pretty good; 13.5% alcohol.

8 **The Best Ribera del Duero 2019** £9.00
Made by major Rioja bodega Muriel, but it's Ribera all the
way: darkly rich and spicy, pure-tempranillo, plummy and
rounded, red-meat wine with grip and length; 14.5% alcohol.

9 **The Best Marques de los**
Rios Rioja Reserva 2017 £9.25
Sweetly ripe and rounded with cassis richness alongside the
vanilla bloom from two years in oak, this has an expensive
quality evoking ice cream with a lick of syrup – in a good way;
13.5% alcohol. Smart Rioja for this money.

RED WINES

SPAIN

🍷 8 Matsu El Picaro 2022 £10.00

From the Toro region, overshadowed by neighbour Ribera del Duero and the source of good wines at more sensible prices, a young, unoaked pure tempranillo with rugged minty-cassis flavours of convincing weight and balance; 14.5% alcohol. The portrait of the young man in the flat cap on the label refers, I guess, to the brand name El Picaro, 'the rogue'.

🍷 8 Contino Reserva Rioja 2017 £26.00

I've tasted this single-vineyard wine, made by Rioja giant CVNE, a number of times, and liked its silky purity, but always wondered about the price. This is a good vintage, well integrating the lush fruit and sweet oak, and drinking pleasurably now; 14% alcohol.

PINK WINES

FRANCE

🍷 9 La Vieille Ferme Rosé 2022 £8.00

Pleasing shell-pink colour; orchard blossom aroma with a hint of strawberry, lively crisp red-fruit freshness that takes a kindly grip of the tastebuds; finishing neatly dry; 12.5% alcohol. Rightfully popular Rhône brand at a sensible price, and it's got chickens on the label. What more could you ask?

🍷 8 Studio Rosé 2022 £14.00

From Provence's filmstar-owned Château Miraval (nice card, Brad) a 'second' wine named in honour of the recording studio installed in the house by a previous proprietor, Jacques Loussier, this is a fine floral refresher that I believe is the equal of the *grand vin*, at a price more in tune with its value; 12.5% alcohol.

PINK WINES

🍷 8 Vitis Nostra Pinot Noir Rosé 2022   **£6.25**
Lombardy party pink with aromas and savours true to the cherry-raspberry pinot noir style, partnering softness with a decent definition of fruit; 11.5% alcohol.

WHITE WINES

🍷 8 The Best Uco Valley Chardonnay 2022   **£10.00**
From scale producer Zuccardi, an impactful Mendoza wine showing ripe sweet-apple fruit in the proper chardonnay tradition with mountain minerality and a supple, leesy richness suggesting oak ageing; convincing; 13% alcohol.

🍷 9 The Best Grüner Veltliner 2021   **£10.00**
Vivid gingery-melon nose and exotic fruit-salad freshness finishing pretty dry combine to make this very distinct aromatic aperitif wine by a fine Niederösterreich producer, Markus Huber, a really rather special treat; 12.5% alcohol.

🍷 8 Cono Sur Bicicleta Viognier 2022   **£7.50**
I think Cono Sur, a brand of Chilean behemoth Concha y Toro, adopted its bicycling theme as a virtue signal: its workers pedal everywhere instead of roaring around in gas-guzzling trucks. But I don't hold this against them. Cono Sur is a safe bet. This one balances tropical viognier fruit-salad ripeness with spiky freshness, full of interest; 13.5% alcohol.

WHITE WINES

9 **La Vieille Ferme Blanc 2022** £8.50

I just can't fault this perennial brand from ace Rhône winemaker Perrin, deliciously ripe with stone- and orchard-fruit savours in this thrilling new vintage, lifted by textbook citrus acidity. It's a genuine any-occasion choice; 12.5% alcohol. It's sold (along with its red and pink counterparts) by most of the supermarkets, very often at useful discounts.

9 **The Best Viognier 2021** £8.50

A brisk one from the Languedoc, it has the right white-nut and preserved apricot richness lifted by twangy citrus acidity; 13% alcohol. Good value. The lexicographic label is fine, but troublingly similar to the style of Majestic's in-house Definition range.

8 **The Best Muscadet 2022** £8.75

This famous Loire-estuary wine can be eyewateringly green and acidic (to its credit, say some devotees) but here's a mild-mannered one, nicely fresh and briny but with ripe-fruit charm, finishing brisk rather than sharp; 12.5% alcohol. Liked it.

10 **The Best Vouvray 2021** £11.00

Luscious chenin blanc from the great Loire Valley appellation of Vouvray has a trace of honey amid the ripe white stone-fruit savours and a lovely lift of limey acidity to finish; 12% alcohol. I am completely taken in, and it's a bargain.

8 **The Best Alsace Pinot Gris 2021** £11.00

From the ubiquitous Turckheim co-operative a full-fat smoky sweet-pear and spice PG in the true Alsace tradition; nice introduction to the style, which deserves to be better known; 13% alcohol.

WHITE WINES

8 **The Best Touraine Sauvignon Blanc 2022** £10.00
Touraine is the handle for sauvignon blanc from its true homeland, the Loire Valley. A lot of the wines made under this generic heading are terrific, like this grassy gooseberry zinger, twanging with freshness and green fruit; 13% alcohol.

8 **Fete Picpoul de Pinet 2022** £10.00
Full-flavour spin on this trendy Mediterranean dry wine. It's packed with eager orchard fruit, suggestions of salinity and evident sunny ripeness; perhaps all this warrants the elevated price; 13% alcohol.

8 **Rigal Vin Orange 2021** £10.50
I've heard 'orange' is a current informal description for 'natural' wines – made without the use of unnatural ingredients such as cultured yeasts, sulphur products or clarifying agents – so the name of this Gascon dry white presaged to me the equivocal delights of cloudiness and alien fruit flavours. But no, while it does have an untypical pale-amber colour (the crushed gros manseng grapes were fermented on their skins, most unusually today for white wines) it's a likeably fresh, crisp and balanced aromatic food wine, no doubt a good partner for vegan dishes; 12% alcohol. Occasionally on offer at £7.

8 **The Best Alsace Gewürztraminer 2021** £11.00
Rose petals, lychees and ginger all suggest themselves on the nose of this well-coloured aromatic spicy just-short-of-sweet conversation piece, a fine aperitif as well as a match for charcuterie, Asian cuisine, blue and other pongy cheeses (especially Alsace's own Munster); 13.5% alcohol. Good example by ubiquitous Turckheim co-operative, of a unique wine style.

WHITE WINES

8 **Louis Jadot Mâcon Villages 2021** £15.00

Jadot is a very big outfit in Burgundy that nevertheless makes many wines of real character. This one is true to the Mâconnais style: orchardy-floral perfume, delicately green tinge to the keen chardonnay flavours, lick of richness (though no oak) and fine balance; 12.5% alcohol.

8 **The Best Petit Chablis 2020** £14.00

Petit Chablis is the humblest of the four rankings of this great appellation at the northern extreme of the Burgundy region, but it can still be counted on to make lovely chardonnays in the true regional style. This is mineral, just short of austere but full of exciting gunflint aromas and stony Chablis freshness; 12.5% alcohol.

8 **The Best Chablis 2020** £16.00

Proper Chablis by ubiquitous UVC co-op for Morrisons; flinty but full and sunnily ripe; 12.5% alcohol. Price has escalated from last year, but I paid £9 on multibuy.

9 **The Best Pouilly Fumé 2022** £18.00

Ultimate Loire Valley Sauvignon Blanc; janglingly zingy, grassy and lush in this new vintage; long saline flavours, complex and stimulating, and I believe well worth the price; 13% alcohol.

WHITE WINES

FRANCE

🍷 10 The Best Chablis Premier Cru 2020 £20.00

Morrisons gets all three of its 'Best' Chablis lines (see above for the other two) from the Union des Viticulteurs de Chablis, the famous appellation's biggest co-operative and supplier of own-label wines to most UK supermarkets as well as under its own brands UVC and La Chablisienne. It's remarkable, I feel, that Morrisons' Chablis bottlings seem so particularly consistent. This 1er Cru is the pick: lemon-gold colour with a green trace, scintillating flinty aroma, lush Chardonnay fruit, mineral and yet rich (some oak contact), Chablis through and through; 12.5% alcohol. I got a bottle for £13.50 on promo – great bargain.

ITALY

🍷 9 Morrisons Soave 2022 £4.99

Remarkably good yet again in this new vintage, the colour's mellow, the nose apple-fresh and inviting, the fruit crisp with the keynote almondy lick and the finish briskly limey; light, 11% alcohol, and very cheap.

🍷 8 The Best Trentino Pinot Grigio 2022 £8.00

Of the four Italian PGs tasted on the day, I liked this one a clear best. Crisp and gently smoky with forward white fruits and a nifty tang; 12.5% alcohol.

🍷 8 The Best Soave Classico 2022 £7.75

Good typical colour with flashes of green in the pale gold, and a recognisable balance between green fruit and elusive blanched-almond richness; 12% alcohol.

WHITE WINES

🍷 9 The Best Verdeca 2021   £8.50

Terrific fresh Puglian dry wine from local grape variety Verdeca with lemon-meringue aromas and layered orchard-citrus-figgy flavours; partly fermented in oak, it has a lingering, luxury aftertaste besides; 12.5% alcohol. Stands out for interest as well as distinctiveness. It's made by Puglia/Campania co-op Cantine San Marzano, which is unrelated to the currently fashionable plum-tomato species. Just so you know.

🍷 8 Gordon Ramsay Vibrante Bianco 2021   £10.00

I thought this might be a leg-pull, but it does conform to the description vibrant white, a Tuscan blend of chardonnay with rather more regionally appropriate varieties vermentino, trebbiano and pecorino, to make a fresh and moderately nuanced dry wine for pasta occasions and celebrity followers; 12.5% alcohol.

🍷 8 The Horologist Sauvignon Blanc 2022   £10.00

Yes, I have time for this, it says in my note. Such a wit. It also says vivid grassy-lemony Marlborough wine with likeable purity and weight; 13% alcohol.

🍷 8 Yealands Sauvignon Blanc 2021   £10.00

This brightly zingy gooseberry-green-pepper refresher from thoroughly dependable Marlborough producer Yealands is a fine flag-waver for the modern Kiwi-sauvignon style; distinct sherbet and lime notes; 12.5% alcohol. Fair price on shelf at Morrisons and I paid only £5.25. It was reduced to £7, and a 25%-off multibuy did the rest.

WHITE WINES

Y 8 The Best Vinho Verde 2021 £8.75
Laid-back variation on the theme with discreet prickle of spritz, bright blossom aromas and appreciable apple-vegetal savours with a lemon lift, and not too sweet at the finish; 12% alcohol.

Y 8 Klein St Sauvignon Blanc 2022 £7.00
I'm glad to see Morrisons persisting with these Klein St wines from the Western Cape, as they're reliably characterful and good value. This is full of ripe green sauvignon fruit, eager grassiness and long flavours; 12% alcohol.

Y 8 64 Edge Sauvignon Blanc 2022 £8.50
Rather lush, it says in my note, meaning, I guess, that it's your exotic sauvignon style, full of green fruit heft and long on the aftertaste; 12.5% alcohol.

Y 8 Septimo Sentido Verdejo 2022 £8.75
Verdejo's the joyous grape variety and the rest of the name translates as the 'seventh sense' – possibly intuition – which I guess explains the bizarre messianic message of the label. Don't be put off, it's a fine peary-grassy characterful dry white of refreshing zest; 12% alcohol.

**Y 8 The Best Marques de los Rios Rioja
Blanco 2022** £9.00
An entirely different animal to the reserva version immediately below, this brisk dry modern white Rioja by Bodega Muriel is good of its kind: fresh white-fruit flavours plumped with a trace of oak slickness and a tangy citrus edge; 13% alcohol.

WHITE WINES

**Y 9 The Best Marques de los Rios Rioja
Blanco Reserva 2016** £13.00

I paid just £7.50 for this. It was reduced to £10 on individual offer and by a further 25% on multibuy. Terrific mature oxidative pure viura with a creamy white-burgundy-with-spearmint nose, lush sweet-orchard fruit and naughty plumpness edged by limey twang. It remained deliciously stable in the fridge for four days after first opening – an enduring treat; 12.5% alcohol. The only supermarket white Rioja of this admirably old-fashioned kind.

FORTIFIED WINES

Y 9 Morrisons 10-Year-Old Tawny Port £15.00

The price of this perennial standby has risen alarmingly, no doubt thanks to the big lift in excise duty, but it's as delicious as ever. Just turning a little orange (tawny) at the edge of the ruby colour, seductively honeyed and figgy with a keen fieriness to balance; 20% alcohol.

Y 10 The Best Palo Cortado Sherry 37.5cl £6.50

Morrisons' range of three premium sherries in half bottles is a wonder. This one's my favourite – but the accompanying Oloroso and Pedro Ximenes are equally delicious on their own terms – and a wine of sublime quality. Made by esteemed Jerez bodega Emilio Lustau it is as dry as the label indicates (all proper sherry is dry) and piquantly poised in aroma and savour, evoking nuts and preserved fruits to delectable effect. The world's best aperitif wine to serve well-chilled in a modestly sized stemmed glass; 19% alcohol. Seems perpetually to be reduced from the risible £6.50 shelf price to a nugatory £5.50.

SPARKLING WINES

ENGLAND

🍷 10 The Best English Sparkling Wine 2010   £27.00
Fair enough, this is indeed the best English sparkling wine I've tasted all year. Fully foaming and formed mature chardonnay with pinots noir and meunier from top UK producer Nyetimber, it's extravagantly mellow and perfectly poised for freshness and lingering fruit flavours; 11.5% alcohol. I believe this spent six years on its lees before disgorgement. The 2011 vintage will follow, and the augurs are good. The price is wholly merited.

FRANCE

🍷 8 Champagne Charles Clément Brut   £24.00
Like this, a new name to me, best for interest and value among several branded Champagnes tasted on the day: fine ethereal weight with gentle lemon twang, elegant and fresh; 12.5% alcohol.

🍷 8 The Best Champagne Brut   £27.00
This is Morrisons' house Champagne, made by Boizel, a well-liked family-owned maison whose wine style has been compared to Veuve Clicquot. Welcoming brioche aroma and creamy mousse with brisk grapefruit note; 12% alcohol.

ITALY

🍷 8 Ferrari Brut   £20.00
Admirable pure-chardonnay Champagne-method sub-Alpine sparkler; crisply, even fiercely, refreshing; distinctively good; 12.5% alcohol. Established in Italy for 120 years, it's finally catching on here since adoption as Formula 1's official winners-rostrum fizz.

Sainsbury's

 Sainsbury's is standing still. Well, in the wine line, anyway. I don't know about the bigger picture.

But Sainsbury's seems quite well situated for stasis. It's the supermarket that really invented supermarket wine, long ago introducing the first recognisable own-label range. It was reported in the *Which? Wine Guide 1982* that the 200 stores were selling one in every six bottles consumed at home in Britain. In that same edition, Tesco wasn't even mentioned.

Well, that was then. Maybe it doesn't matter that Sainsbury's got left behind. There are still good wines to be had, particularly from the Taste the Difference own-label range, accounting for most of the 30-odd wines I've picked out this year. I have bought all of them from the stores, pouncing during the fairly frequent price promotions that continue to prevail.

Highlights include Taste the Difference Château Les Bouysses Cahors 2020 at £13.00. It's a wonder of the range, consistent vintage after vintage, and I hope it will continue to be a flagbearer for the characterful and historic red wines of Cahors.

Good wishes, too, for Taste the Difference Jurançon Sec 2021 at £8.00, a rare bird from Pyrenean France I liked so much I featured it on my occasional slot on Channel Four's *Sunday Brunch* show. A newish addition to the Sainsbury's list, I hope equally fervently it will last the distance.

RED WINES

ARGENTINA

9 **Alamos Malbec 2021** £9.75
From leading Mendoza producer Catena, a generic varietal of sleek sour-cherry ripeness plumped with oak contact into a plush partner for meaty menus; 13.5% alcohol.

8 Taste the Difference Fairtrade
Morador Malbec 2021 £9.00
Generously ripe and pruny long-serving Sainsbury's stalwart from admirable Fairtrade-affiliated Casa del Rey winery in Mendoza; has good black-fruit intensity and friendly grip; 13.5% alcohol.

AUSTRALIA

9 Taste the Difference Château Tanunda
Barossa Cabernet-Merlot 2021 £14.00
That the Tanunda estate styles itself a château is a clue to the Bordeaux style of this shimmering cassis, cedar and summer-berry fruits offering, silky from oak contact and trimmed with friendly tannins; 14.5% alcohol. That this distinguished winery (est 1890, the oldest in the Barossa) has for so long supplied this wine to Sainsbury's is quite a tribute to the excellent Taste the Difference range.

CHILE

8 Taste the Difference Chilean Pinot Noir 2021 £8.50
A full-fruit style to this mellow red-summer-fruits pinot from the Bio-Bio, one of Chile's cooler climes; good complete food wine (poultry and game come to mind) with gentle grip and spice; 13.5% alcohol.

RED WINES

FRANCE

8 Taste the Difference St Chinian 2019   £9.50

From one of the more distinctive appellations of the Languedoc, this well evokes the rocky high-country location of St Chinian with its garrigue aromas of wild thyme and bristly rosemary, fruits-of-the-forest savours and sun-baked ripeness; 14% alcohol.

8 Cru des Côtes du Rhône Villages
Vinsobres 2020   £10.50

Roasty nose to this dark, peppery and very ripe superior CdR from what was clearly a hot year in the vineyards. Baked summer fruits, sinewy texture and and liquorice intensity (14.5% alcohol) make it a winter wine to go with starchy or meaty comfort foods. Not for the faint-hearted. I paid £7.50 on promo.

8 Taste the Difference Ventoux 2020   £10.50

Particularly ripe and spicy vintage for this epic Rhône Valley appellation famously centered on Mont Ventoux, a gruelling mountain stage of the Tour de France; intense black (and red) berry fruits with grip and dark savours; 14.5% alcohol.

9 Taste the Difference Beaujolais Supérieur 2021 £11.00

I'm not convinced the designation *supérieur* has any real meaning as a Beaujolais appellation, but I do like the classic purply, juicy, bouncy and vivid character of this wine by 150-year-old producer Mommessin. Stands out and the price is sensible, especially at what I paid for it: £6 on promo; 12.5% alcohol.

RED WINES

FRANCE

9 Taste the Difference Château Les Bouysses Cahors 2020 £13.50

A consistent wonder of the Sainsbury's offering, this is a richly silky and warmingly spicy all-malbec oak-matured wine from the famous appellation of Cahors in the Lot Valley, deep in rustic south west France. The story goes that wine has been made at Les Bouysses since the year 1230, and I'm inclined to believe it. This vintage is succulent and rounded, sweetly savoury and 13.5% alcohol.

GERMANY

9 Taste the Difference Rheinhessen Pinot Noir 2021 £8.00

Given how ruthlessly Sainsbury's has been pruning the Taste the Difference range of late, I'm impressed by the longevity of this oddball red from Germany. It looks (paleish ruby) smells (sweet strawberry and red cherry) and tastes (juicy, bright, new-squished summer red-fruits) more like red Burgundy (from the Chalonnais, I'll venture) but it really is German, and I think it's lush; 12% alcohol. Will chill well on warm days.

ITALY

8 House Montepulciano 2021 £5.50

Sainsbury's budget 'House' range is not always a treasure trove but this decently integrated brambly Abruzzo wine is wholesomely ripe; 12.5% alcohol.

8 Taste the Difference Primitivo 2022 £8.25

This standby Puglian pure-varietal has plumpness and spiciness in agreeable tandem, darkly brambly with blueberry notes, trim at the finish; 13.5% alcohol.

RED WINES

ITALY

🍷 8 **Taste the Difference Marzemino 2021**   £9.75
Hardy perennial from sub-Alpine Trentino and one of that elusive breed – red wines that suit chilling. This has inky-dark colour but an easy, obliging weight of fruit – think raspberry, bramble, sour cherry – and a near-austere grippiness that gives it a great cut for serving with rich food including sticky pasta or risotto; distinctively delicious; 12.5% alcohol.

🍷 8 **Taste the Difference Vino Nobile di Montepulciano 2018**   £12.00
A sort of super-Chianti, usually terribly expensive, this is a very decent Vino Nobile of intense colour and ritzy cassis-sour-cherry fruit, poised and slinky, nice and edgy; 13.5% alcohol. Terrible labelling, but I promise the price is modest - in context.

SPAIN

🍷 8 **Cune Crianza Rioja Tempranillo 2020**   £7.50
Vigorous blackcurrant one-year-in-oak wine identifiably of the Rioja family, darkly sinewy and grippy; you could keep this for years and await mellow developments or enjoy it with meaty treats right now; 13.5% alcohol.

🍷 8 **Taste the Difference Cepa Alegro Rioja Reserva 2017**   £9.50
Smooth and mellow it avers on the back label of this hardy Sainsbury's perennial, but I thought it sinewy and stern. An arrestingly closed-up Rioja of evident quality but in need of longer bottle-ageing or, in case of emergency, decanting well in advance; 13.5% alcohol.

RED WINES

SPAIN

8 Taste the Difference CVNE Ribera del Duero Roble 2020 £10.50

Robust, textured pure Tempranillo with dark blackcurrant savours slicked by six months in oak, very much in the Ribera del Duero style although made by Rioja bodega CVNE; 14% alcohol. This is a wine still young, and worth decanting. It should develop for years in bottle. Good investment.

8 Taste the Difference Old Vine Garnacha 2020 £10.50

New to me, this is a muscular and dark plummy baked-fruit monster (15% alcohol) from north east Spain's Calatayud region, famed for super-ripe garnacha reds. It's tempered by a certain sour-cherry juiciness and lifting acidity, finishing brisk; grows on you.

PINK WINES

FRANCE

8 Taste the Difference Fronton Negrette Rosé 2021 £7.50

Fronton is an out-of-the-way vine zone near Toulouse in darkest south west France and negrette the local grape variety that makes some good, deeply coloured pink wines like this one. It has crisp red-berry juiciness and an easy acidity, finishing dry and clean; 12.5% alcohol.

WHITE WINES

ARGENTINA

9 Alamos Chardonnay 2021 £9.00

From top Mendoza producer Catena, this new incarnation under the Alamos label – the name that put Argentina on the 'everyday' wine map back in the 1980s – is a generic varietal but a swish one: generous colour, creamy crisp-apple scent and corresponding lush flavours; 13.5% alcohol. Very easy to like, and well worthy of the Catena name.

WHITE WINES

8 **Taste the Difference Austrian Riesling 2021** £10.00

AUSTRIA

Floral scents to this peachy but recognisably racy riesling in the aromatic Austrian manner lead on to nectareous apricot and sweet apple fruit flavours lifted by keen citrus twang; a distinctive spin on the great riesling grape by Markus Huber, Austrian winemaking royalty; 12.5% alcohol.

8 **Star Gazer Sauvignon Blanc** £6.25

CHILE

Zippy bargain, artfully balanced between floral aromatics and grassy vivacity; Chilean sauvignon has charms all its own – including competitive value; 12% alcohol.

10 **Taste the Difference Jurançon Sec 2021** £8.00

Top marks to Sainsbury's for listing this off-beat dry wine from between Lourdes and the Pyrenees. Jurançon is best known for its lush 'dessert' wines from late-harvested gros and petit manseng grapes. This is an earlier-picked blend with lavish colour and a proper basket of citrus and orchard fruit aromas giving on to assertive, generous and zesty corresponding flavours, finishing crisp and bright. Top aperitif and a natural match for poultry as well as fish and summer salads. Good white for winter drinking too; 13% alcohol.

FRANCE

9 **Taste the Difference Côtes du Rhône Blanc 2022** £8.00

Bright gold colour, inviting spring-blossom scent and heady peachy-nutty white fruits combine to make this excellent contrivance by Rhône star Gabriel Meffre a perennial marvel. Dry, fresh food wine of a complexity that makes it look underpriced; 13% alcohol.

WHITE WINES

GERMANY

🍷 **9** **Taste the Difference Pfalz Pinot Blanc 2021** **£7.75**
Terrific Rhine (Pfalz) spin on the theme of Alsace Pinot Blanc, this has intriguing blossom aroma, lush apple and pear fruit, crisp minerality and a nifty twang of citrus acidity; a racy version of the better-known original from the other side of the Alps; 12.5% alcohol.

ITALY

🍷 **8** **Taste the Difference Soave Classico 2022** **£8.00**
This is no shrinking violet – a very full-flavoured rendering of the crisp appley Veronese stalwart dry white but still with plenty of lively freshness and lemon tang; 12.5% alcohol.

NEW ZEALAND

🍷 **8** **Taste the Difference Coolwater Bay**
Sauvignon Blanc 2022 **£9.50**
Zingy Awatere Valley refresher by admired Yealands Estate; it has green-pepper aromas and crunchiness, grassy lushness and satisfying length balanced by correct limey acidity; 13% alcohol.

🍷 **9** **Taste the Difference Pinot Gris 2021** **£10.50**
The clue is in the name Pinot Gris. This is an aromatic, lushly exotic but dry wine in France's Alsace tradition. It's the same grape as the pinot grigio of Italy, but a world apart. Made by Yealands, it's a revelation: smoky and spicy tropical-fruit scents and savours, lifting citrus twang, lovely balance; 13% alcohol.

SPAIN

🍷 **8** **Taste the Difference Albariño 2021** **£9.50**
Pioneering own-label Rias Baixas on good form, zesty ocean-breeze freshness to the grassy, lush white fruits finishing citrussy crisp but long and lip-smacking; 13% alcohol.

SPARKLING WINES

9 **Louis Pommery Sparkling Wine England Brut**   £26.00
Yes, English fizz from a Champagne producer, Vranken-Pommery (formerly Pommery & Greno est 1836) who established a vineyard in Hampshire in 2017 and are already in the market. This is very like Champagne from Champagne. Same grapes – mainly chardonnay plus pinots meunier and noir – same method of production and same thrill of streaming bubbles bearing lush biscuity orchard fruits in vivid abundance; 12.5% alcohol. Good price, too, undercutting Pommery's domestic brands.

9 **Taste the Difference Crémant de Loire Brut**   £12.00
Beguiling blend of chenin blanc and chardonnay makes up this luxuriant, creamily foaming, apple-peach-brioche, crisply finishing sparkler from Ladubay, one of the Loire Valley's best producers; 12.5% alcohol.

8 **Sainsbury's Champagne Blanc de Noir Brut**   £23.50
Since last year's debacle – a bottle that tasted suspiciously oversugared – I have tried this perennial favourite more than once and found it altered. I won't claim again that it's oversugared – as in too much of the sweet *liqueur de dosage* added at the final corking of the disgorged wine – but I do believe this is no longer the thrillingly balanced champagne it once was. Panic paused, but the price has also risen quite sharply; 12.5% alcohol.

Tesco

Tesco put up 156 of its wines for the 2023 tasting, describing this formidable number as "only a snapshot of the total selection" in what I hope was a spirit of jest. Included were 30 wines "brand new to the range" – "from great-value week-night wines to premium wines for celebrations".

There is an air, you'll gather, of enthusiastic optimism in the Tesco wine department. Tasting the wines, it's easy enough to see why. This range is certainly wide, and deep. I find for example that I have recommended five different white wines from Spain – I couldn't leave any of them out, too good, but to come across this many best buys in what is a relatively obscure market niche is an indicator worth remarking on.

Among the five maximum-scorers in this Tesco line-up I must mention the non-vintage Finest Châteauneuf du Pape (£21). It is a one-off blend of wines from several estates within this grand Rhône appellation and from at least four different vintages. It is phenomenally good, and I am promised that there will be enough of it in the stores to last into 2024, but devotees of CdP will be wise, I suggest, to shop early.

Another quirky item to catch my eye was Les Terrasses St Nicolas de Bourgueil 2022 (£9.50). It is a red wine from the Loire Valley, where the cabernet franc makes distinctive leafy-juicy-grippy wines of great character. They are on the whole neglected by the supermarkets, but here's Tesco making this very fine one a featured addition to the list in 2023.

Good omens. And finally, a reminder about Tesco discounting. As far as I can tell, the frequent reductions on wine prices – usually 25% off selected bottles or the whole range on a multibuy basis – are now exclusively targeted at Clubcard holders. If you wish to get acquainted with Tesco wine, get a Clubcard without delay.

RED WINES

ARGENTINA

8 **Viñalba Reserve Cabernet Sauvignon 2021**   £11.00
Confidently made, ripe dark style with the classic Bordeaux grape; an impressive job of replicating the elegant restraint of serious claret; fascinating sleek wine apparently made without oak contact, very natural in its richness; 14.5% alcohol.

9 **Finest The Trilogy Malbec 2019**   £13.00
Unexpectedly callow colour, but this is a grown-up wine by serious Mendoza producer Catena that delivers a full-bore, expensively upholstered mouthful of silky berry-fruit pure malbec, sweetly ripe but very trim at the finish; flagship wine at a fair price; 13.5% alcohol.

AUSTRALIA

10 **d'Arenberg The Footbolt Shiraz 2021**   £12.50
I've been following this McLaren Vale classic for ever. It's named, the story goes, after a racehorse called The Footbolt, beloved of its owner, Joseph Osborn, who nevertheless sold it in 1912 to fund the purchase of the d'Arenberg vineyard. Happily an Osborn descendant, Chester, is still in the saddle, and has made this 107th anniversary vintage, which is the best I've tasted yet. Colour is gloriously opaque, sumptuously perfumed, the fruit intense, blackly savoury, cushiony but well-knit, rounded and utterly delicious; 14.5% alcohol. Safe bet.

8 **Hardys Tintara Cabernet Sauvignon 2021**   £12.00
Hardys, the name on a billion bottles of Aussie plonk, seems to be branching out. This McLaren Vale cab-merlot blend has deep maroon colour, intense blackcurrant aromas and corresponding pure, focused fruit of perfectly judged weight and balance; 14% alcohol. Grown-up wine.

RED WINES

AUSTRALIA

🍷 **9** **Wynns The Siding Cabernet Sauvignon 2021** **£15.50**
This famed Coonawarra producer's pure cabernet has a glowing intense beetroot colour and, I've written down here, refined, elegantly weighted, slinky blackcurrant fruit. Yup, I liked it. And a wine to last; drink now for a real treat or keep for years; 13.7% alcohol.

BULGARIA

🍷 **8** **Zlato Valley Merlot 2021** **£4.50**
Natural-tasting black-cherry party wine from the Mediterranean-like climate of Bulgaria's Thracian Lowlands, it says here. Nice try; 12% alcohol.

CHILE

🍷 **8** **Lateral Pinot Noir** **£4.29**
Cherry-bright non-vintage party red you could happily chill; brisk but integrated, and very cheap; 13% alcohol.

🍷 **8** **Finest Block 18 Cabernet Sauvignon 2019** **£8.00**
Restrained Colchagua blend (one-tenth cabernet franc) by Cono Sur. Brambly charm and leafy liveliness as well as convincing intensity of ripe berry fruit with evident silk from oak contact, benefitting from bottle age; 13.5% alcohol. Works for me.

🍷 **8** **LFE Gran Reserva Leyda Valley Pinot Noir 2022** **£10.50**
Grippingly good, earthy pinot in the best Chilean tradition, brimming with sunny ripeness and wholesomely tight at the edge; fine match for chicken and duck dishes; 14% alcohol.

RED WINES

FRANCE

⊻ 9 **Finest Côtes du Rhône Villages Signargues 2022 £8.50**
Great big liquorous CdR of exceptional ripeness, still
wholesome in weight and balance with sweet spice and trim
grippy edge to the burgeoning berry fruit; 14.5% alcohol.
Signargues, southernmost of the Rhône's named top villages,
won its AC in 2005.

⊻ 8 **Finest Saint-Chinian 2021**   **£9.00**
From a remote appellation of rugged Mediterranean hill
country, a spicily ripe fruits-of-the-forest winter red of
genuine territorial character. Particularly good in this vintage;
13.5% alcohol.

⊻ 9 **Les Terrasses St Nicolas de Bourgueil 2022   £9.50**
This excitingly good Loire Valley red from cabernet franc
grapes has benchmark leafy-stalky freshness to the lush red-
berry fruit and an intensity suggesting it will age gracefully – a
hallmark of the wines of the prestigious St Nicolas de Bourgueil
appellation; 12.5% alcohol. Loire reds respond well to gentle
chilling.

⊻ 8 **Paul Mas Languedoc 2022**   **£10.00**
Slick Mediterranean blend of syrah, grenache and mourvèdre
has intensity of black berry and currant fruits expressed in
long, spicy, baked savours; 13.5% alcohol.

⊻ 8 **La Burgondie Moulin-à-Vent 2020**   **£12.50**
This tastes like posh Beaujolais, and that's exactly what it is.
Juicy blue-tinged fresh strawberry-raspberry fruits lifted by
crisp acidity and with a generous plumpness; 12.5% alcohol.

RED WINES

🍷 **8** **Lirac Arbousset 2020**   **£12.50**

Lirac is a near neighbour to Châteauneuf du Pape in the southern Rhône and produces comparable wines at more sensible prices. This slick and spicy discreetly oaked winter wine tastes as grand as it looks and will develop in the bottle for years; 14.5% alcohol.

🍷 **10** **Finest Châteauneuf du Pape**   **£21.00**

What, no vintage? This is fabulously good so I had to ask. Charlotte Lemoine, who looks after Tesco's French range, explained to me that this bottling is a blend of several vintages including 2016, 17, 20 and 21, in quantities too small to make single-dated cuvées, but a very fine mix all together. It's a masterpiece: rich, earthy and sweet with hedgerow fruit, warm spice, plum, damson and sour cherry notes; drinking perfectly right now; 14.5% alcohol.

🍷 **8** **Finest Margaux 2018**   **£22.00**

I was honoured to taste this vaunting claret produced for Tesco by *Troisième Grand Cru Classé* estate Château Boyd-Cantenac. And it does taste the part: complex cassis, cedar and liquorice aromas and savours, creamy richness (14 months in Bordeaux barriques, up to half of them new), perfect poise and balance; 14% alcohol. One important proviso: I'd give it several more years to come round in the bottle before it will drink at its best.

🍷 **7** **Vista Castelli Montepulciano d'Abruzzo 2021**   **£5.35**

Last time, the 2020 vintage was one of my wines of the year. This 2021 isn't a patch: juicy but lean and possibly drying out; 12.5% alcohol.

RED WINES

ITALY

🍷 9 **Finest Montepulciano d'Abruzzo 2021** £7.00
Intense but perky brambly spaghetti red with focus and juicy brightness, all in fine balance; it's palpably well-made and tastes well above its price; 13.5% alcohol.

🍷 9 **Finest Chianti Classico Riserva 2019** £9.25
I have found much variation in the vintages of this long-serving brand by jumbo producer Melini but this one scores well. It's sleek, elegant and mature-tasting with proper sour-cherry piquancy as well as nutty creaminess from oak contact; 13.5% alcohol. Good price for serious Chianti.

🍷 8 **Campo V Primitivo de Manduria 2019** £16.00
Wow – a big, rich hit of baked black fruit on nose and palate from this extraordinary Puglian plum-damson monster might leave you wondering whether it's sweet or just overpowering. A good match probably with something roasted, or with loud cheese. It does finish very dry and tight; 15.5% alcohol.

🍷 8 **Finest Amarone Valpolicella 2019** £18.50
Gorgeous jewel-like colour, coffee, chocolate and conserved fruits on the pungent nose but it's not sweet, it's *amarone* meaning 'bitter' in description of this admirable style of Valpolicella made with the addition of super-concentrated must; this is a well-executed example of the genre and at a fair price; 15.5% alcohol.

SOUTH AFRICA

🍷 8 **Kleine Zalze Shiraz Cabernet Sauvignon 2020** £9.00
Impactful toasty black-fruit cassis-and-spice in this warming Cape blend is delivered in a pleasingly sinewy medium with poise and completeness; an impressive match for meaty menus; 14.5% alcohol.

RED WINES

SOUTH AFRICA

🍷 **8** **Bellingham Pinotage 2020** £11.00
This proper rendering of the Cape's indigenous hybrid grape is plump with just the faintest suggestion of trademark tarriness and a little mint lift amid the dark, liquorous intensity; good partner to spicy dishes as well as roast meats; 14% alcohol.

SPAIN

🍷 **8** **Casa Maña Tempranillo 2022** £4.25
Jolly party red by mega producer Felix Solis in Spain's La Mancha; juicy with brambly-cassis fruit and healthily plump, finishing brisk; 11.5% alcohol.

🍷 **9** **Finest Viña del Cura Rioja Reserva 2018** £10.00
A worthy succcessor to the brilliant 2017, it's darkly defined in its cassis-raspberry ripeness with the slick oak smoothness nicely in harmony; reserva Rioja every inch of the way, in the modern manner with the fruit to the fore; it might well develop further in bottle; 13.5% alcohol.

🍷 **9** **Finest Ribera del Duero 2020** £12.00
Spain's river of gold rises in the Ribera del Duero and flows a hundred miles and more west to the frontier with Portugal where it becomes the Douro of Port country. And now the Ribera itself aspires to world-class winemaking: sleek reds like this delicious pure tempranillo from happily named Bodegas Portia, founded in 2010 with a winery designed by Sir Norman Foster, no less. It's a sumptuous maroon-colour cassis-vanilla-warm-spice gripper of noble charm; 14.5% alcohol.

RED WINES

USA

🍷 **8** **Bonny Doon Vineyard Le Cigare Volant 2020** **£18.00**
This is a Caifornian nod to Châteauneuf de Pape in France's Rhône Valley where in the 1950s local worthies placed a ban on the landing of alien spacecraft (*cigares-volants*) in the vineyards. The Bonny Doon version employs Rhône grape varieties to make this relatively light but spicily savoury and gripping tribute; 13.5% alcohol. Quirky and fun.

PINK WINES

FRANCE

🍷 **9** **Caves des Roches Coteaux d'Aix en Provence 2022** **£7.50**
My pick of the pinks this year, it has attractive smoked salmon colour, floral/fruit-blossom nose, crisply defined red-berry juiciness with proper pink savours. Dry, as it should be, and realistically priced even though in a silly wiggly-shaped bottle I thought had been extinct for a generation, it's as good as I reckon rosé needs to be; 12.5% alcohol.

🍷 **8** **Finest Côtes de Provence Rosé 2022** **£10.00**
Shell pink, quite soft on entry but the red fruits are crisp and it's fresh – and fun; 13% alcohol.

🍷 **9** **Arbousset Tavel Rosé 2021** **£12.50**
Tavel in the Côtes du Rhône is a major rosé appellation but not as prominent here as it was before the competition from Provence came to the fore. Try this one: standout strawberry colour with juicy berry fruits, closer to red wine than other pinks, generous but dry and brisk; 13.5% alcohol. Dare I say rosé of the old school, and that gets a high mark.

PINK WINES

8 Kylie Minogue Côtes de Provence Rosé 2022   £16.00
I was inclined to be sniffy about this celebrity-signature pink from vineyards 'wholly orientated around maximising quality and environmental sustainability' but it's objectively pretty good. Pale onion-skin colour, delicate red-berry aromas and fruits, lush but poised, nicely lifted by citrus zing; 12.5% alcohol. Expensive, but that's showbiz for you.

8 Wairau Cove Rosé 2022   £8.50
Pale onion-skin colour, dry near-austere style but you get the raspberry-cherry charm of the pinot-noir-led fruit (the rest is merlot) and a citrus lift to finish; 12.5% alcohol. Kiwi pinks compete well for interest and value.

8 Ramon Bilbao Rioja Rosado 2022   £9.00
Garnacha grapes steeped with their skins for just the right extraction of colour and savour make for an attractive dry rosé with real fruit flavours that will match well with most menus; nicely done; 12% alcohol.

WHITE WINES

8 Finest Torrontes 2022   £8.00
Torrontes is Argentina's indigenous white grape, thriving at very high Andean altitude. Try this one, made by top local producer Catena, for size: dry and lively with hints of muscat grapiness, ginger and rose petal trimmed with bright citrus acidity; 12.5% alcohol. Well-made niche wine at a sensible price.

WHITE WINES

8 Finest Western Australian Sauvignon
Semillon 2022 £9.00

Crisp, just short of austere, dry but generously fruity and really rather poised wine on what might be based on the model of Bordeaux blanc (same grape varieties) works really well as an aperitif; 12.5% alcohol.

AUSTRALIA

8 Finest Tingleup Riesling 2022 £11.00

Old favourite from Howard Park and very good in this ripe vintage – sweet apple and raisin notes but very dry, limey and mineral; 13% alcohol.

8 d'Arenberg The Broken Fishplate
Sauvignon Blanc 2022 £12.50

Tesco has a good little range of wines from the Adelaide Hills winery of d'Arenberg, celebrated for serious wines with silly names. This is a luscious tangy distinctly nuanced very dry sauvignon with the faintest suggestion of pétillance - great fun, at a price; 12.5% alcohol.

10 Finest Valle de Leyda Chardonnay 2022 £8.50

Viva Chile! From well-rated Leyda Valley by big outfit Luis Felipe Edwards, a richly coloured and ripe unoaked pure varietal with Chablis-like struck-match flintiness to the complex, nuanced and lush sweet-apple, peach and lime fruit, finishing squeaky clean and fresh; 13.5% alcohol. Irresistibly good and good value.

CHILE

8 Cono Sur Reserva Especial Riesling 2022 £10.00

Generous in the Alsace-riesling style with a limey twang in the Aussie-riesling style, this is nothing like German riesling. Ripe, plump, mineral and really quite dry; 13% alcohol. Nifty match for exotic menus.

WHITE WINES

🍷 8 Finest Côtes de Gascogne 2022 £7.50
Very likeable racy, limey, dry, anytime wine by formidable
Producteurs Plaimont full of refreshment and interest and just
11.5% alcohol.

🍷 8 Finest Picpoul de Pinet 2022 £9.50
Fuller in fruit and weight than some picpouls, which is fine,
a dependable perennial, fresh and tangy in this vintage;
13% alcohol.

🍷 9 La Burgondie Mâcon-Villages 2022 £11.00
A real find – lush but unoaked, sunnily ripe southern Burgundy
plump with ripe and minerally classic Mâconnais chardonnay
from a prolific and particularly ripe vintage; 12.5% alcohol.

🍷 8 Finest Pouilly-Fumé 2022 £15.00
Lovely in this vintage – steely-fresh, seagrass-lush, long-
flavoured pure sauvignon blanc from one of the Loire Valley's
top appellations; 13% alcohol. I much preferred it this year to
its counterpart Finest Sancerre (same producer) at £15.

🍷 9 Finest Chablis 2021 £14.50
Instantly recognisable Chablis from its gunflint chardonnay
nose and matching mineral fruit, gloriously generous in apple-
crisp, fleetingly minty fruits with fine green acidity, beautifully
balanced; 12% alcohol. A much better buy than the Finest
Chablis 1er Cru at £17 from the same producer (although 2020
vintage).

🍷 9 Finest Mosel Steep Slopes Riesling 2022 £7.00
Trim and tangy classic racy refreshing riesling marrying sweet-
apple ripeness to zingy citrus acidity; fine refreshing delicate
aperitif dry wine and a bargain price; 11% alcohol.

FRANCE

GERMANY

WHITE WINES

GERMANY

🍷 **9** **Schloss Vollrads Riesling Trocken 2021** £13.00
This dry (*trocken*) and beautifully weighted ripe riesling from a fabled 13th-century estate has elevated mineral raciness and startling crispness; 11% alcohol. World class aperitif wine at what seems a perfectly reasonable price.

ITALY

🍷 **8** **Finest Passerina 2022** £7.00
Abruzzo dry wine has fresh, vegetal aromas, nectarine and orchard fruits, from distinctive passerina grape, delicate but memorable; 13% alcohol.

🍷 **10** **Finest Soave Classico Superiore 2021** £8.25
Nice green-gold colour and brassica nose on this decidely superior Veronese classic dry white – edgily fresh but with a lick of blanched-nut creaminess furthered by up to a year in oak casks; an artful contrivance and a proper treat at this price; 13% alcohol. I am completely taken in.

NEW ZEALAND

🍷 **8** **Wairau Cove Pinot Grigio 2022** £7.50
If you like pinot grigio from Italy, try this. From Gisborne and Hawkes Bay on NZ's North Island, it sings with the aromatic, smoky, white-fruit friskiness that marks out this delectable grape variety; lovely exotic dry wine that matches every kind of menu from salad to spicy, fish to white meats; 12% alcohol.

🍷 **8** **Finest Marlborough Sauvignon Blanc 2022** £9.50
Classic Kiwi gooseberry style with grassy-nettly rush of freshness and citrus twang – familiar, stimulating and very likeable; 12% alcohol.

WHITE WINES

NEW ZEALAND

8 Babich Classic Sauvignon Blanc 2022 £13.00
The Babich family, immigrants from war-torn Dalmatia (Croatia) in the early 1900s, were pioneers of New Zealand winemaking, and remain among the best of them. The first, astonishing Kiwi wine I can remember trying was a Babich sauvignon of about 1985. Try this more recent triumph: big-flavoured, glitteringly vivid, nettly and leesy-sherbetty green-fruit refresher of serious intent; 12% alcohol.

8 Finest North Row Vineyard Sauvignon Blanc 2021 £13.00
Premium Marlborough wine by Villa Maria with lush intensity and pebbly freshness perhaps in the style of grand Loire appellations like Sancerre; it's impressive and fascinating; 14% alcohol.

SOUTH AFRICA

8 Finest Stellenbosch Chenin Blanc 2022 £7.50
Quite a bracing style overall to this distinctive pure varietal in spite of partial fermentation in French oak barriques. Trademark chenin blanc honey/blossom notes come through on nose and palate and there's a true lemon tang; 13.5% alcohol.

8 Finest Western Cape Sauvignon Blanc 2022 £7.50
Easy to like this crisp and grassy green-apple refresher. Cape sauvignons often score for matching ripeness to freshness and this fits the bill at a sensible price; 12% alcohol.

SPAIN

8 Casa Maña Chardonnay 2022 £4.09
Workmanlike La Mancha chardonnay with sweet green notes amid the convincing ripeness, fresh and wholesome, and all at an inexplicable price; 11.5% alcohol.

WHITE WINES

SPAIN

9 **Finest Viña del Cura Rioja Blanco 2022** £9.00
It has spent four months ageing in American oak, and you can tell. Luscious but refreshing nod to the white Rioja of old (now mostly edged out by steely modern bone-dry confections), full of interest and the perfect match for fishy paella, barbecues, everything; 13% alcohol.

8 **Finest Viñas del Rey Albariño 2022** £11.00
Vivacious seaside-breezy Galician very-dry and tangy refresher; lots of ripe crunchy white-fruit savour, satisfying and uplifting; 12.5% alcohol.

8 **El Jardin de Ana Godello 2021** £10.00
Green but lush Galician pure godello; sea-breeze savoury with a sherbet dab, serious and delicious; 12.5% alcohol.

8 **Mar de Frades Albariño 2021** £17.00
The tall azure bottle might well attract your eye, and the contents don't disappoint. Top of the range Rias Baixas classic has fine lemon-gold colour, expansive ocean-fresh aromas and flavours, very dry and very satisfying; 12.5% alcohol.

SPARKLING WINES

ENGLAND

8 **Finest English Sparkling Brut** £21.00
From happily named Hush Heath estate in Kent, this enthusiastically sparkling champagne-grape blend combines apple crispness with creamy, yeasty richness; 12% alcohol.

SPARKLING WINES

8 **Finest 1531 Blanquette de Limoux 2020** £10.00
Distinctive full-fizz sparkler from the Pyrenees; vividly fresh
and bristling with crisp orchard-fruit flavours, briskly dry and
satisfying, and all at a very sensible price; 12.5% alcohol.

10 **Finest Premier Cru Champagne Brut** £25.00
Completely consistent quality at a perpetually fair price, this
is easily the pick of all supermarket own-label Champagnes.
It is sourced from rated 'premier cru' vineyards in the rightly
venerated Côte des Blancs south of Epernay where much of the
chardonnay harvest goes into prestige cuvées. It shows. Lovely
sunny colour, warm yeasty aroma, crisp white fruits, fresh and
exciting; 12.5% alcohol. The price is up drastically from last
year's £21, but there are regular Clubcard discounts.

FRANCE

Waitrose

Waitrose (& Partners) sails serenely on. The great edifice that is owner John Lewis (& Partners) might be wobbling about a bit, but the grocery arm is looking just fine, and that certainly goes for the wine department.

I believe there are more than a thousand wines on the Waitrose list – you'll find a modest proportion in the average store but all of them online for home delivery – and the diversity of the list is beyond compare.

Where to start? There are 70 firmly recommended best buys in the following pages, and you'll see that France is writ large: top-scoring reds include a plain-wrapper Montgravet 2021 (£9.99) from the Hérault and Triguedina Malbec du Clos, an outstanding Cahors (£10.99); among white top picks is a superb Beblenheim co-op Reserve Pinot Gris 2021 (£11.99) from Alsace.

There are just two German wines – Waitrose has easily the best choice – but both are great and great value, and among the burgeoning choice of organic wines I've top-scored perennial favourite Primitivo Terre de Fiano 2021 (£9.99) from Italy's Puglia and Reyneke Chenin Blanc 2022 (£9.99) from South Africa.

Sherry has always featured strongly at Waitrose and this year there are some new additions. Pedro's Almacenista Oloroso (£11.49) has me in complete thrall. It is a very great dark sherry by any standard, and at a price surely a fraction of the true worth of what is a world-class wine.

Before I get carried away, a reminder that Waitrose's discounting of wines continues apace. There are perpetual promos of up to third off dozens of individual lines and occasional blanket deals of 25% off everything. There's even a five per cent discount if you buy more than six bottles at a time, any time.

RED WINES

ARGENTINA

♈ 9 Waitrose No 1 Malbec 2020   **£14.99**
This one hits the spot. Intense deep crimson colour, full-frontal, richly oaked but ideally balanced, black-fruit ripeness in the best Mendoza manner tasting vivid, lipsmacking and powerful; 14.5% alcohol. Memorable.

♈ 9 Norton Malbec Reserve Finca Agrelo 2021   **£15.99**
Slick, sumptuous and seductive, a big spicy smoothie for big, beefy occasions; 14.5% alcohol. Waitrose Cellar (online) only.

AUSTRALIA

**♈ 9 Thistledown Summer Road Old Vine
       Grenache 2022**   **£9.49**
Pale in the way of some Rhône grenache and middling in weight this nevertheless has real poise and savour – sunny spice in the squishy red fruits with impressive balance; 14% alcohol. It's from the Riverland region of South Australia but could easily be mistaken for its French model.

♈ 8 Jip Jip Rocks Shiraz 2021   **£12.99**
Soupy but cleverly judged blackberry blockbuster from Padthaway; well-poised, delivering gently spiced cushiony ripe savours with length and firmness at the finish; 14% alcohol.

♈ 8 Jim Barry The Forger Shiraz 2020   **£24.99**
This top-drawer Clare Valley wine is definitely the real thing: full, complete special-occasion wine from opaque crimson colour to lipsmacking plum-spice-black-berry fruit and trim ripe-tannin edge; 14% alcohol.

RED WINES

FRANCE

8 Sous Le Soleil du Midi Merlot 2022 £6.99
Impressionistically presented Mediterranean summertime red with plenty of juicy black-cherry merlot fruit but it's artfully balanced for brightness at the finish; 13.5% alcohol.

9 Château Capendu La Comelle 2020 £8.99
The colour is intense, deep crimson and the nose blooms with blackberry ripeness; fruit is opulent but juicy, hinting at creaminess but grippy at the finish; a true Languedoc blend of grenache, carignan and syrah with trademark spice and sun-bake; 14% alcohol. Serious value from Jean-Claude Mas, a prolific supplier of generic Languedoc wines to UK supermarkets ("Mas-production" quip the wine-trade wags), but also a cool hand at characterful single-estate productions such as this handsome Corbières.

8 Cellier des Dauphins Costières de Nîmes 2022 £8.49
Perky purple bramble and white-pepper mainly syrah rustic Rhône picnic red under a big but responsible brand; vigorous and juicy; 13% alcohol.

10 Montgravet 2021 £8.99
This plain-wrapper screwtop Pays d'Hérault (Languedoc) is a revelation. It's entirely Carignan – at most usually a blending grape – from a vineyard planted 40 years back and it is truly distinctive: wild aromas of redcurrant and bramble, raspberry and cherry, middling weight of crunchy red corresponding fruits, fine texture and balance; 12.5% alcohol.

RED WINES

8 **Le Malbec de Balthazar 2022** £9.49

Limpid crimson colour and a sweet brambly nose invite you into this poised Languedoc-Roussillon wine's very ripe and gently spicy black fruit, edged with firm but friendly soft tannins; 13% alcohol. A likeable alternative to Argentine malbec and a versatile food matcher.

9 **Rémy Ferbras Ventoux 2020** £9.49

The appellation of Ventoux, on the Provence-Rhône border, is centred on the stark, volcano-like mountain notorious as a tough stage of the Tour de France cycling route, now a rightly popular watch on ITV4. I'm glued to it, and hope that UK sales of Ventoux wines are benefitting accordingly. This one is quite distinct among Rhône reds, with a juicy cherry-raspberry lift to the warm, sage-and-spice red fruits and wholesome plumpness – it's 14.5% alcohol and wears it lightly. The maker clearly has an eye on the British market: among the food matches suggested on the back label is shepherd's pie. This wine is regularly on promo at just £6.99 – a gift.

9 **Château du Père Antoine Blaye 2018** £9.99

Good intensity of ruby colour, sweet violet/black cherry pong and plenty of fully ripe, even mellow, black fruit from this merlot-led maturing claret of humble appellation – Côtes de Bordeaux – but aspiring depth and length; 13.5% alcohol. Rarely good claret at this price.

8 **Vignerons Ardèchois Syrah Les Classiques 2021** £10.49

The Ardèche, north of Provence and south of the Rhône Valley is a vinous backwater, but here's a worthy introduction: bright plummy (skin-on) spicy midweight with juiciness and piquancy to match meaty and starchy menus; 12.5% alcohol.

FRANCE

RED WINES

10 Triguedina Jean-Luc Baldès Malbec du Clos 2019 £10.99

This is Cahors, a beautiful town and significant appellation of the Lot Valley 100 miles east of Bordeaux that has for centuries made one of France's most distinctive red wines. Trouble is, Cahors has fallen out of fashion, swept away on the tide of 'varietal' wines named for their constituent grape variety, not their place of origin. This wine identifies as malbec, with the AC as an afterthought, but it is a true Cahors, sinewy and spicy in its dense black-fruit glory, rounded and full of savour, finishing with fine ripe tannins; 14% alcohol.

8 Mas des Montagnes Côtes du Roussillon Villages 2016 £11.99

Classy Pyrenean syrah-grenache blend; sleek, fruit-fleshy and mineral, and benefitting from years in bottle as well as ageing in oak; 14.5% alcohol. Producer Lorgeril, est 1620, is a dependable name. I got it for £9.49.

8 Sirius 2018 £12.49

Generic Bordeaux, 6 parts merlot to 4 cabernet sauvignon and commands attention from first sniff. Fine silky aroma of heady black fruits and corresponding ripe, structured savours; maturing wine that may develop further; 14% alcohol.

8 Dominique Piron Beaujolais-Villages 2021 £13.99

Potent perfume and joyous juiciness abound in this purple bouncer full of new-squished redcurrant-raspberry gamay fruit; 12.5% alcohol. Expensive but certainly delicious; consider chilling it gently.

RED WINES

FRANCE

8 **L'Empreinte Rouge Lirac 2021** £13.99

Gutsy grenache-syrah-mourvèdre blend from a dependably distinctive Cru of the Côtes du Rhône, Lirac. This has dark and profound black-fruit depths and a seductive silkiness - a style regularly compared to Châteauneuf du Pape, just 10km distant. Good match for game; 14.5% alcohol. I paid £9.74 on promo.

8 **Chorey-Les-Beaune Joseph Drouhin 2020** £23.99

This elegant red Burgundy by grand grower/merchant Drouhin is still young and tannic but lush and silky too with piquant pinot fruit artfully enriched by time in oak; 13.5% alcohol. Safe bet for a special occasion – especially a year or two in the future.

9 **Les Charmes de Grand Corbin St-Emilion**
Grand Cru 2012 £24.99

Sweet, gently spirity, pleasantly decaying mature St-Emilion; turning a little orange at the rim in its second decade and tasting silkily earthy and ripe; it's an absolute treat; 13% alcohol.

GERMANY

9 **Louis Guntrum Pinot Noir 2020** £14.99

Smart move by Rheinhessen winery Guntrum to sell this as pinot noir rather than under the German name for the grape, spätburgunder. It's a fine cherry-coloured and -scented pure-fruit pinot of poise and healthy weight comparable to Burgundy and competitive in price; 13.5% alcohol.

RED WINES

GREECE

9 Atma Xinomavro 2021 £12.49

The colour and heft of this pure xinomavro, native, and principal, grape of northern Greece, is very reminiscent of pinot noir and you even get the strawberry scent and savour of the (unrelated) pinot in this one's elegant, juicy midweight fruit, nicely tied together with friendly tannins; 13% alcohol. Distinctively serious wine.

ITALY

8 Loved & Found Lacrima Marche 2021 £8.99

Deep maroon colour to this hearty Ancona wine resolves into a focused, juicy fruitiness with a quirky elderberry note, dark and satisfying, finishing dry and brisk; 13% alcohol.

10 Terre di Faiano Organic Primitivo 2021 £9.99

The enthusiasm with which Waitrose has promoted sales of this Puglian phenomenon throughout the year worries me. What if it sells out? I'm not sure I could do without it. The 2021 vintage, well up to scratch, was still on shelf as this book went to press, but if the 2022 follows, I won't hesitate. Made by the appassimento method – with the inclusion of ultra-ripe grapes in the ferment – the wine is broodingly dark, sweetly perfumed of roses, chocolate and minty herbs, bursting with ripe sun-baked blackberry fruit; extraordinary and delicious; 13.5% alcohol. Versatile food-matcher, unmistakable in its orange livery. Oh, and very frequently, so far, on discount.

8 Venturina Freisa d'Asti 2022 £10.99

Big whiff of cassis syrup on the nose of this Piedmont wine from obscure Freisa grape variety leading on to a surprisingly restrained, if vigorous, brambly fruit comparable in style with better-known red Barbera d'Asti. I liked this paleish juicy red for its clean cut and brisk freshness; 12.5% alcohol.

RED WINES

🍷 8 Santa Tresa Rina Russa Organic
Frappato 2022 £10.99

The colour is barely more intense than rosé, but it's red wine right enough, from Sicily, perky with bright redcurrant/cherry juiciness of wholesome sweetness and artful balance, dry and flattering to fishy dishes as well as pastas, barbecues, you name it; 13% alcohol. Don't fear serving it cool.

🍷 9 Stemmari Passiata Rosso 2021 £10.99

Darkly delicious nicely rounded berry-fruit Sicilian, partly from the island's indigenous nero d'avola grape but mostly syrah (native to the Rhône) this satisfyingly plump pasta red has glowing ripeness ideally balanced by brisk acidity; 13.5% alcohol. Grows on you.

🍷 8 Masi Campofiorin 2019 £14.99

One-off Verona wine with a winning label design, in effect a Valpolicella variant based on the popular lightweight pasta red's sour-cherry breeziness, pumped up with concentrated must from store-dried bunches to create a plush but piquant special-occasion red of real heft complete with marzipan richness and Christmas-cake savours, finishing keen and tight; 13% alcohol.

🍷 8 Chateau Oumsiyat Mijana 2019 £9.49

A blend of cabernet sauvignon with Rhône/Midi varieties syrah, carignan and cinsault, this sturdy fascinator from the Bekaa Valley – home to world-renowned Chateau Musar – has the baked-fruit warmth that characterises the region's reds and savoury spiciness to the plummy-blackberry depths; 13% alcohol. A conversation piece from a nation that needs our business.

ITALY

LEBANON

RED WINES

🍷 **8** **The Sardine Submarine Red 2021** £7.99

Portugal loves a sardine, and I guess this enjoyable everyday wine from the Tejo, Lisbon's littoral, would make a nice match for a few of these fine little fishes. Sweetly ripe but wholesomely clean-finishing blend with gently spicy red and black berry fruits; 12.5% alcohol. The name, incidentally, is after the yellow trams that have plied the old streets of Lisbon since 1901.

🍷 **8** **Loved & Found Trincadeira 2021** £8.99

Darkly savoury food wine from Alentejo region neighbouring Lisbon with herby notes to the rich fruit (and some oak contact) edged with sweet tannin; 13.5% alcohol.

🍷 **8** **Reyneke Organic Cabernet Sauvignon Merlot 2020** £9.99

The inviting sun-warmed blackcurrant nose on this oak-matured Western Cape blend leads into poised fruit savours in the restrained Bordeaux style, edged with ripe tannins; 14% alcohol.

🍷 **9** **Journey's End Sir Lowry Cabernet Sauvignon 2019** £14.99

The vineyard for this Stellenbosch straight cabernet is neighbour to a eucalyptus forest and I like to believe the minty-resiny suggestion in the supple, lush black savours of the sleekly oaked (some new cask) maturing finished product is connected; 14% alcohol. I do like Waitrose's own description: 'richly curvaceous wine ... dark plum, chocolate and spice flavours'. And finally, the name Sir Lowry commemorates Irish born General Sir Galbraith Lowry Cole, who served as Governor of the Cape Colony from 1825–33.

RED WINES

SPAIN

10 **Marques de Calatrava Reserva**
Tempranillo 2015 **£8.99**

From La Mancha, the great plain (and wine lake) of central Spain, this has the browning colour and relishably decaying aroma of an old wine (which it is) from the grander Rioja region (same grape) at a bargain price. Still plenty of cassis savour here alongside the creamy vanilla from oak contact, really quite convincing; 13.5% alcohol.

USA

8 **American Gothic Lodi Zinfandel 2021** **£9.99**

Grant Wood's alarming 1930 portrait 'American Gothic' of farmers and their lancet-windowed frame house provides the label for this jolly and not particularly rustic blueberry/black cherry Californian wine; sweet but not confected and a bit of solemn fun; 14% alcohol.

PINK WINES

FRANCE

8 **Le Bijou de Sophie Valrose 2022** **£9.99**

I liked the 2021 and this is its equal, pale and delicate rosé from the obscure Coteaux de Béziers zone of the Languedoc, with elegant strawberry freshness to the crisp fruit and easy acidity; 12.5% alcohol. Sophie Valrose was a local *vigneron* of long ago, fondly remembered for championing quality wine – and the rights of women workers.

8 **Alaina Rosé 2022** **£12.99**

From busy Laurent Miquel in the Hérault, brisk and bright cinsault-syrah blend; firm berry fruits and positive freshness; tastes pink, and that counts for a lot; 12.5% alcohol.

PINK WINES

8 **Loved & Found Organic Nerello Mascalese 2022** £8.99

Attractive smoked-salmon colour, crisp floral perfume, fresh and nuanced delicately set summer red fruit savours in this impressive dry Sicilian wine; 12% alcohol. Waitrose wine buyer Poppy de Courcy-Wheeler explains the absence of a capsule on the bottle: 'The removal of capsules means this wine will help to reduce half a tonne of unnecessary packaging per year'.

WHITE WINES

9 **Waitrose Blueprint Grüner Veltliner 2022** £8.99

From the rather self-effacing own-label range (although with an improved new blue-label style this year, I note) this is a fine and good-value rendering of Austria's flagship aromatic grape. Exotic with hints of muscat and white pepper, but dry, it has the power to partner all sorts of awkward menus, including spicy, salady, smoky and fishy; 12.5% alcohol.

8 **Domaine Huber Grüner Veltliner 2022** £11.99

I'm including this because tasting it right after the own-label GV above was a good reminder that these wines can be delightfully diverse. This one is much fuller in fruit and weight and even more pungent and exotic in style; dry, though, and another fine food matcher; 12.5% alcohol.

8 **Morandé Terrarum Patrimonial Semillon 2022** £9.99

The semillon grape, known for golden Sauternes and Aussie exotics, here makes a dry but luscious wine with melon-mango-pineapple notes hefted with the inclusion of must fermented on the skins; the effect is distinctive and enjoyable; 12.5% alcohol.

WHITE WINES

CHILE

8 Santa Carolina Reserva Sauvignon Blanc 2022 £9.99
Emphatically a sauvignon in the fuller, riper style, still with tangy gooseberry and grassiness of flavour and finishing with lift and crispness; 13% alcohol.

ENGLAND

7 Waitrose Blueprint English Dry White 2022 £11.49
This brave attempt from Surrey is in style a country wine with homely orchard-blossom scent and matching off-dry fruit; 11.5% alcohol.

FRANCE

8 Le Sauvignon Blanc de Balthazar 2022 £8.99
I like that the vines for this grow within sight of the ancient walls of the fortified city of Carcassonne, deep in the Languedoc. Lots of sunny ripeness nicely balanced by tangy citrus acidity; 12.5% alcohol.

8 Waitrose Touraine Sauvignon Blanc 2021 £9.49
The grassy-nettly zest to this generic Loire Valley dry wine is very easy to like, not too green but fresh and lively; 12.5% alcohol.

10 Paul Mas Réserve Languedoc Blanc 2022 £9.99
The Mas family of Pézenas in the Hérault, a short hop from the Mediterranean, started making wine in 1892 and are now in what I call Mas-production, particularly for UK supermarkets. And the quality, at all levels, is astounding. The current, dashing winemaker is Jean-Claude Mas and he's a phenomenon. This inspired dry white shows how: fine colour, a basket of fruits, orchard, tropical, citrus lifts the aromas, and the mélange of fresh, luscious flavous, generous and with lifting acidity, is pure South of France; 13% alcohol.

WHITE WINES

8 **Laurent Miquel Vendanges Nocturnes**
Viognier 2022 £9.99

The grapes are picked at night at Cazal Viel in Languedoc to prevent the heat of day at harvest time prompting spontaneous fermentation – thus the notably fresh and citrussy style of this fleetingly honeyed and luscious but definitely dry viognier; 12.5% alcohol.

9 **Domaine Vieux Vauvert Vouvray 2021** £10.49

The description 'Medium Dry', prominent on the label of this luscious Loire wine, is misleading. 'Medium' is meaningless and I am certain a major turnoff for most wine lovers. This wine, from the fabled appellation of Vouvray, is dry in the manner of the constituent regional grape chenin blanc. As well as dry it is also lush, not sweet, and not medium. It brims with floral, tangy and juicy savours and is as refreshing as it is nuanced; a fine example of a great dry wine style; 11.5% alcohol.

8 **Vignerons Ardèchois Classiques Viognier 2022** £10.49

While the viognier is known for plump, even soft, white wines, this is dry from the off, still with the gentle preserved-fruit pungency of the style, but pleasingly restrained and fresh; 14% alcohol.

10 **Alsace Pinot Gris Réserve 2021** £11.99

Designated 'medium dry' on the back label, this lush item from the excellent co-operative of the impossibly picturesque Alsace village of Beblenheim is traduced by the description. It's smokily, aromatically dry and evokes ripe fruits including pineapple (fresh cut, not canned) and tangy lime; 13% alcohol. Brilliantly made, truly distinctive in the Alsace style and a great match for tricky dishes like smoked fish, spicy stuff, even salads. Top aperitif wine too. Bargain price, and regularly on discount at £8.99.

WHITE WINES

9 Domaine Masson-Blondelet Pouilly-Fumé 2022 £16.49
Defining sauvignon blanc, it has just the sort of glistening river-pebbly freshness that summons up the lush waterside vineyards of Pouilly-sur-Loire at the heart of the grape's natural homeland. Yardstick zesty nettly perk-you-up classic for special occasions; 13% alcohol.

8 Chatel-Buis Montagny 2022 £16.49
Lushly coloured and ripe all-chardonnay Burgundy from one of the region's outlying appellations, the Côte Chalonnaise; convincing long peachy-nectarine fruits, trim and tangy; 12.5% alcohol.

8 Château de la Mulonnière L'Effet
Papillon Savennières 2015 £18.99
Its lavish gold colour, honeysuckle nose and oxidative style might betoken a sweet wine, but this is a *sec* from the western Loire Valley appellation of Savennières where the chenin blanc grape produces white wines of great variety including dry but succulent delights like this one; a great match for poultry as well as fish; 12.5% alcohol.

8 Marc Dudet Saint-Véran 2021 £21.99
Deluxe but unoaked white burgundy from the Mâconnais; has the region's trademark chardonnay lushness and minerality with a rich leesy egginess full of interest; 13% alcohol.

9 Leitz Rüdesheim Magdalenenkreuz
Riesling Kabinett 2021 £13.99
Lemon-gold colour, floral and sharp-apple aromas, faintest spritz in the body, a lovely balance between honeyed ripeness and racy green-apple tingly Riesling; exciting dry but nectareous Rheingau wine from a great family producer following admirable eco practices in the vineyards; just 9% alcohol.

FRANCE

GERMANY

WHITE WINES

GERMANY

9 Dr Loosen Ürziger Würzgarten Riesling Kabinett 2021 £15.99

Startlingly zesty classic moselle from the great Ernie Loosen; elegant, long-flavoured and perfectly poised between fleetingly honeyed ripe-apple fruit and piquant lemon acidity; fabulous aperitif wine at a fair price for what it is, and just 8% alcohol.

GREECE

8 Zacharias Assyrtiko 2022 £12.49

Florally perfumed dry aperitif wine from the Peloponnese peninsula of south west Greece is fresh, bright and appley with a lick of leesy richness; 14% alcohol.

ITALY

8 Il Grifone d'Oro Soave Classico 2022 £7.99

Soave seems to be everywhere this year – a welcome return to voguishness for this old Veronese favourite. This one has good green-shot colour and a likeable austerity, very brisk white fruits but with a sneaky lick of blanched almond richness; 12.5% alcohol.

8 Waitrose Loved & Found Zibibbo 2022 £8.99

Sicilian just-dry aromatic wine from a grape, Zibibbo, also known as muscat of Alexandria, the constituent of countless 'dessert' wines. This one is full of grapey fruit but refreshing in style with a clear lemon zest, and thoroughly Italian in character; 12.5% alcohol.

9 Eccelsa Vermentino di Sardegna 2022 £9.99

Totally new to me at Waitrose, a very likeable gold-coloured dry but lushly ripe orchard-fruit fresh wine with baked-apple richness balanced by a twang of acidity. It's from prime vineyards on the island of Sardinia, natural home to the excellent vermentino grape; 13.5% alcohol.

WHITE WINES

NEW ZEALAND

🍷 **8** **Otira Sauvignon Blanc 2022** £10.99

New one to me, but made by redoubtable Kim Crawford in Marlborough, a seagrassy, green-pepper zesty refresher with long flavours and tight, tangy finish; 12.5% alcohol.

🍷 **8** **Blind River Sauvignon Blanc 2022** £12.99

Full-fruit style from Marlborough includes about one-tenth of wine fermented in oak barrels; you get plenty of zesty greenness and the extra heft does add something, even if I'm not certain quite what; satisfying as well as refreshing; 13% alcohol.

SOUTH AFRICA

🍷 **10** **Reyneke Organic Chenin Blanc 2022** £9.99

Family producer Reyneke stick to biodynamic principles in winemaking and are members of the Cornerstone project to support their workforce. This wine bears it all out. It's relatively austere for a Cape chenin blanc but this allows a better glimpse of the pure natural ripeness the grape can achieve and somehow you sense it – and there's a gorgeous leesiness in tandem with the limey edge at the finish; special wine; 13.5% alcohol.

🍷 **8** **Paul Cluver Village Chardonnay 2022** £13.99

In effect, this is Cape (well, Elgin Valley) white Burgundy. Pure chardonnay brimming with sweet-apple ripeness and peachy asides, good freshness and minerality with elusive mintiness and trimmed up citrus-crisp; 13% alcohol.

SPAIN

🍷 **8** **Baron de Ley Rioja Blanco 2022** £8.99

I'm always on the lookout for interesting (ie old-fashioned oxidative) white Rioja and this one is no such thing but it's by good outfit Baron de Ley and although dry and bright in the modern style does have some redemptive ripeness; 13% alcohol.

WHITE WINES

SPAIN

8 | Altos de Torona Albariño 2022 £14.99
From Rias Baixas, the Atlantic-facing region of north west Spain where the albariño grapes are grown on high pergolas to maximise exposure to the ocean breezes, this is a fine, leesy, saline and bracing dry green-fruit wine with agreeable ripeness; 13% alcohol.

FORTIFIED WINES

PORTUGAL

9 | Graham's Blend No 5 Port £27.49
Rare and expensive white port; comes in a peculiar ceramic bottle but looks good in a glass – rich gold colour and artfully balanced between sweetness, fieriness and lifting acidity; an exotic aperitif to enjoy well-chilled with a handful of almonds; 19% alcohol.

9 | Waitrose Medium Dry Amontillado Sherry £9.99
In Waitrose's self-effacing Blueprint own-label range, this is crackingly good amontillado beguilingly enriched with a dollop of darkly caramelised pedro ximenes. Fine fruit-cake winter sherry, but do serve it chilled to enjoy the balance of autumnal mellowness and crisp acidity to the full; 18.5% alcohol.

SPAIN

8 | Pedro's Almacenista Selection Fino Sherry £9.99
Fine gold colour to this fresh-tasting dry sherry in a range new to Waitrose this year; it's jangling with brisk preserved fruit flavours, clean-edged, a terrific aperitif to serve well-chilled; 15% alcohol.

10 | Pedro's Almacenista Selection Oloroso Sherry £11.49
Burnished brass colour, bold toasty aroma (*oloroso* means fragrant) and piquant but rich fruit-cake savours paradoxically but delectably dry in style; a lovely sherry style to enjoy in the way of port with cheese and nuts or chilled as an aperitif; 20% alcohol. Outstanding rare sherry at a rare price.

FORTIFIED WINES

9 **Lustau On The QT Fino Sherry 50cl** **£19.99**
Amber gold, wildly pungent fino sherry of lavish deliciousness, bursting with blanched nut and preserved fruit flavours, creamy but dry (not bone-dry though) and truly exciting. If you love sherry, you'll surely fall for this; 15% alcohol. Enjoy thoroughly chilled from small wine glasses. Waitrose Cellar only.

SPARKLING WINES

10 **Waitrose Leckford Estate Brut 2019** **£29.99**
Leckford Estate, a farm and place of recreation owned by Waitrose/John Lewis in Hampshire's dreamy Test Valley, has a vineyard. Each harvest of its chardonnay and pinots noir and meunier grapes are trucked to ace producer Ridgeview in Sussex and turned into this phenomenally good sparkling wine. It's not cheap but it's very much in the full-mousse Champagne tradition, abounding with zesty white fruits, yeasty richness and extravagant ripeness. Quite glorious; 12.5% alcohol.

9 **Waitrose No 1 Brut Special Reserve 2015** **£35.99**
Long-aged and notably mellow Champagne, in the fuller-fruit style, ripe and rounded – a standout vintage wine at a fair price for special occasions; 12.5% alcohol.

9 **Codorniu 1872 Organic Cava Brut** **£10.99**
Proper fully foaming bottle-fermented bready bumper-fruit refresher from Catalonian giant Codorniu. It bears the date 1872 not because it was made in that vintage but in commemoration of the first year cava, Spain's national sparkler, was made. This is a fine fizz with 11.5% alcohol. I've seen it on offer at £7.99 – and that's a real deal.

Enjoying it

Drink or keep?

Wines from supermarkets should be ready to drink as soon as you get them home. Expensive reds of recent vintage, for example from Bordeaux or the Rhône, sold as seasonal specials, might benefit from a few years' 'cellaring'. If in doubt, look up your purchase on a web vintage chart to check.

Some wines certainly need drinking sooner than others. Dry whites and rosés won't improve with time. Good-quality red wines will happily endure, even improve, for years if they're kept at a constant moderate temperature, preferably away from bright light, and on their sides so corks don't dry out. Supermarkets like to advise us on back labels of red wines to consume the product within a year or two. Pay no attention.

Champagne, including supermarket own-label brands, almost invariably improves with keeping. Evolving at rest is what champagne is all about. Continue the process at home. I like to wait for price promotions, buy in bulk and hoard the booty in smug certainty of a bargain that's also an improving asset. None of this applies to any other kind of sparkling wine – especially prosecco.

Of more immediate urgency is the matter of keeping wine in good condition once you've opened it. Recorked leftovers should last a day, but after that the wine will oxidise, turning stale and sour. There is a variety of wine-saving stopper devices, but I have yet to find one that works. My preferred method is to decant leftovers into a smaller bottle with a pull-cork or screwcap. Top it right up.

Early opening

Is there any point in uncorking a wine in advance to allow it to 'breathe'? Absolutely none. The stale air trapped between the top of the wine and the bottom of the cork (or screwcap) disperses at once and the 1cm circle of liquid exposed will have a negligible response to the atmosphere. Decanting the wine will certainly make a difference, but whether it's a beneficial difference is a matter for conjecture – unless you're decanting to get the wine off its lees or sediment.

Beware trying to warm up an icy bottle of red. If you put it close to a heat source, take the cork out first. As the wine warms, even mildly, it gives off gas that will spoil the flavour if it cannot escape.

Chill factor

White wine, rosé and sparkling wines all need to be cold. It's the law. The degree of chill is a personal choice but icy temperatures can mask the flavours of good wines. Bad wines, on the other hand, might benefit from overchilling. The anaesthetic effect removes the sense of taste.

Red wines can respond well to mild chilling. Beaujolais and stalky reds of the Loire such as Chinon and Saumur are brighter when cool, as is Bardolino from Verona and lighter Pinot Noir from everywhere.

Is it off?

Once there was a plague of 'corked' wine. It's over. Wine bottlers have eliminated most of the causes. Principal among them was TCA or trichloroanisole 123, an infection of the raw material from which corks are made, namely the bark of cork oak trees. New technology developed by firms such as Portuguese cork giant Amorim has finally made all cork taint-free.

TCA spawned an alternative-closure industry that has prospered mightily through the supply of polymer stoppers and screwcaps. The polymer products, although unnecessary now that corks are so reliable, persist. They're pointless: awkward to extract and to reinsert, and allegedly less environmentally friendly than natural corks.

Screwcaps persist too, but they have their merits. They obviate the corkscrew and can be replaced on the bottle. They are recyclable. Keep them on the bottles you take to the bottle bank.

Some closures will, of course, occasionally fail due to material faults or malfunctions in bottling that allow air into the bottle. The dull, sour effects on wine of oxidation are obvious, and you should return any offending bottle to the supplier for a replacement or refund. Supermarkets in my experience are pretty good about this.

Wines that are bad because they are poorly made are a bit more complicated. You might just hate it because it's not to your taste – too sweet or too dry, too dense or too light – in which case, bad luck. But if it has classic (though now rare) faults such as mustiness, a vinegar taint (volatile acidity or acetate), cloudiness or a suspension of particles, don't drink it. Recork it and take it back to the supplier.

Glass action

There is something like a consensus in the wine world about the right kind of drinking glass. It should consist of a clear, tulip-shaped bowl on a comfortably long stem. You hold the glass by the stem so you can admire the colour of the wine and keep the bowl free of fingermarks. The bowl is big enough to hold a sensible quantity of wine at about half full. Good wine glasses have a fine bevelled surface at the rim of the bowl. Cheap glasses have a rolled rim that catches your lip and, I believe, materially diminishes the enjoyment of the wine.

Good wine glasses deserve care. Don't put them in the dishwasher. Over time, they'll craze. To maintain the crystal clarity of glasses wash them in hot soapy water, rinse clean with hot water and dry immediately with a glass cloth kept exclusively for this purpose. Sounds a bit nerdy maybe, but it can make all the difference.

What to eat with it?

When tasting a hundred or more wines one after the other and trying to make lucid notes on each of them, the mind can crave diversion. Besides describing the appearance, aroma and taste, as I'm supposed to do, I often muse on what sort of food the wine might suit.

Some of these whimsical observations make it into the finished reports for this book. Like all the rest of it, they are my own subjective opinion, but maybe they help set the wines in some sort of context.

Conventions such as white wine with fish and red with meat might be antiquated, but they can still inhibit choice. If you only like white wine must you abstain on carnivorous occasions – or go veggie? Obviously not. Much better to give detailed thought to the possibilities, and go in for plenty of experimentation.

Ripe whites from grapes such as Chardonnay can match all white meats, cured meats and barbecued meats, and most saucy meat dishes too. With bloody chunks of red meat, exotic whites from the Rhône Valley or Alsace or oaky Rioja Blanco all come immediately to mind.

As for those who prefer red wine at all times, there are few fish dishes that spurn everything red. Maybe a crab salad or a grilled Dover sole. But as soon as you add sauce, red's back on the menu. Again, the answer is to experiment.

Some foods do present particular difficulties. Nibbles such as salty peanuts or vinegary olives will clash with most table wines. So buy some proper dry sherry, chill it down and thrill to the world's best aperitif. Fino, manzanilla and amontillado sherries of real quality now feature in all the best supermarkets – some under own labels.

Eggs are supposed to be inimical to wine. Boiled, fried or poached certainly. But an omelette with a glass of wine, of any colour, is surely a match. Salads, especially those with fruit or tomatoes, get the thumbs-down, but I think it's the dressing. Forgo the vinegar, and salad opens up a vinous vista.

Cheese is a conundrum. Red wine goes with cheese, right? But soft cheeses, particularly goat's, can make red wines taste awfully tinny. You're much better off with an exotic and ripe white wine. Sweet white wines make a famously savoury match with blue cheeses. A better match, I believe, than with their conventional companions, puddings. Hard cheeses such as Cheddar may be fine with some red wines, but even better with a glass of Port.

Wine with curry? Now that incendiary dishes are entirely integrated into the national diet, I suppose this is, uh, a burning question. Big, ripe reds such as Australian Shiraz can stand up to Indian heat, and Argentine Malbec seems appropriate for chilli dishes. Chinese cuisine likes aromatic white wines such as Alsace (or New Zealand) Gewürztraminer, and salsa dishes call for zingy dry whites such as Sauvignon Blanc.

But everyone to their own taste. If there's one universal convention in food and wine matching it must surely be to suit yourself.

———A Wine Vocabulary———

A brief guide to the use of language across the wine world – on labels, in literature and among the listings in this book

A

AC – *See* Appellation d'Origine Contrôlée.

acidity – Natural acids in grape juice are harnessed by the winemaker to produce clean, crisp flavours. Excess acidity creates rawness or greenness; shortage is indicated by wateriness.

aftertaste – The flavour that lingers in the mouth after swallowing or spitting the wine.

Aglianico – Black grape variety of southern Italy. Vines originally planted by ancient Greek settlers from 600BC in the arid volcanic landscapes of Basilicata and Cilento produce distinctive dark and earthy reds.

Agriculture biologique – On French wine labels, an indication that the wine has been made by organic methods.

Albariño – White grape variety of Spain that makes intriguingly perfumed fresh and tangy dry wines, especially in esteemed Atlantic-facing Rias Baixas region.

alcohol – The alcohol levels in wines are expressed in terms of alcohol by volume ('abv'), that is, the percentage of the volume of the wine that is common, or ethyl, alcohol. A typical wine at 12 per cent abv is thus 12 parts alcohol and, in effect, 88 parts fruit juice. Alcohol is viewed by some health professionals as a poison, but there is actuarial evidence that total abstainers live shorter lives than moderate consumers. The UK Department of Health declares there is no safe level of alcohol consumption, and advises that drinkers should not exceed a weekly number of 'units' of alcohol. A unit is 10ml of pure alcohol, the quantity contained in about half a 175ml glass of wine with 12 per cent alcohol. From 1995, the advisory limit on weekly units was 28 for men and 21 for women. This was reduced in 2016 to 14 for men and women alike.

Alentejo – Wine region of southern Portugal (immediately north of the Algarve), with a fast-improving reputation, especially for sappy, keen reds from local grape varieties including Aragones, Castelão and Trincadeira.

Almansa – DO winemaking region of Spain inland from Alicante, making inexpensive red wines.

Alsace – France's easternmost wine-producing region lies between the Vosges Mountains and the River Rhine, with Germany beyond. These conditions make for the production of some of the world's most delicious and fascinating white wines, always sold under the name of their constituent grapes. Pinot Blanc is the most affordable – and is well worth looking out for. The 'noble' grape varieties of the region are Gewürztraminer, Muscat, Riesling and Pinot Gris and they are always made on a single-variety basis. The richest, most exotic wines are those from individual *grand cru* vineyards, which are named on the label. Some *vendange tardive* (late harvest) wines are made, and tend to be expensive. All the wines are sold in tall, slim green bottles known as flûtes that closely resemble those of the Mosel. The names of producers as well as grape varieties are often German too, so it is widely assumed that Alsace wines are German in style, if not in nationality. But this is not the case in either particular. Alsace wines are dry and quite unique in character – and definitely French.

amarone – Style of red wine made in Valpolicella, Italy. Specially selected grapes are held back from the harvest and stored for several months to dry them out. They are then pressed and fermented into a highly concentrated speciality dry wine. Amarone means 'bitter', describing the dry style of the flavour.

amontillado – *See* sherry.

aperitif – If a wine is thus described, I believe it will give as much pleasure before a meal as with one. Crisp, low-alcohol German wines and other delicately flavoured whites (including many dry Italians) are examples.

appassimento – Italian technique of drying out new-picked grapes to concentrate the sugars. Varying proportions of appassimento fruit are added to the fermentation of speciality wines such as amarone and ripasso.

Appellation d'Origine Contrôlée – Commonly abbreviated to AC or AOC, this is the system under which top-quality wines have been defined in France since 1935. About a third of the country's vast annual output qualifies across about 500 AC (or AOP – see Appellation d'Origine Protégée) zones. The declaration of an AC on the label signifies that the wine meets standards concerning location of vineyards and wineries, grape varieties and limits on harvest per hectare, methods of cultivation and vinification, and alcohol content. Wines are inspected and tasted by state-appointed committees.

Appellation d'Origine Protégée (AOP) – Under European Union rule changes, the AOC system is gradually transforming into AOP. In effect, it means little more than the exchange of 'controlled' with 'protected' on labels. One quirk of the rules is that makers of AOP wines will be able to name the constituent grape variety or varieties on their labels, if they so wish.

Apulia – Anglicised name for Puglia, Italy.

Aragones – Synonym in Portugal, especially in the Alentejo region, for the Tempranillo grape variety of Spain.

Ardèche – Region of southern France to the west of the Rhône river, home to a good IGP zone including the Coteaux de l'Ardèche. Decent-value reds from Syrah and Cabernet Sauvignon grapes, and less interesting dry whites.

Arneis – White grape variety of Piedmont, north-west Italy. Makes dry whites with a certain almondy richness at often-inflated prices.

Assyrtiko – White grape variety of Greece now commonly named on dry white wines, sometimes of great quality, from the mainland and islands.

Asti – Town and major winemaking centre in Piedmont, Italy. The sparkling (spumante) wines made from Moscato grapes are inexpensive and sweet with a modest 5 to 7 per cent alcohol. Vivid red wine Barbera d'Asti also produced.

attack – In wine-tasting, the first impression made by the wine in the mouth.

Auslese – German wine-quality designation. *See* QmP.

B

Baga – Black grape variety indigenous to Portugal. Makes famously concentrated, juicy reds of deep colour from the grapes' particularly thick skins. Look out for this name, now quite frequently quoted as the varietal on Portuguese wine labels.

balance – A big word in the vocabulary of wine tasting. Respectable wine must get two key things right: lots of fruitiness from the sweet grape juice, and plenty of acidity so the sweetness is 'balanced' with the crispness familiar in good dry whites and the dryness that marks out good reds. Some wines are noticeably 'well balanced' in that they have memorable fruitiness and the clean, satisfying 'finish' (last flavour in the mouth) that ideal acidity imparts.

Barbera – Black grape variety originally of Piedmont in Italy. Most commonly seen as Barbera d'Asti, the vigorously fruity red wine made around Asti – once better known for sweet sparkling Asti Spumante. Barbera grapes are now cultivated in South America, producing less-interesting wine than at home in Italy.

Bardolino – Once fashionable, light red wine DOC of Veneto, north-west Italy. Bardolino is made principally from Corvina Veronese grapes plus Rondinella, Molinara and Negrara. Best wines are supposed to be those labelled Bardolino Superiore, a DOCG created in 2002. This classification closely specifies the permissible grape varieties and sets the alcohol level at a minimum of 12 per cent.

Barossa Valley – Famed vineyard region north of Adelaide, Australia, produces hearty reds principally from Shiraz, Cabernet Sauvignon and Grenache grapes, plus plenty of lush white wine from Chardonnay. Also known for limey, long-lived, mineral dry whites from Riesling grapes.

barrique – Barrel in French. *En barrique* on a wine label signifies the wine has been matured in casks rather than tanks.

Beaujolais – Unique red wines from the southern reaches of Burgundy, France, are made from Gamay grapes. Beaujolais nouveau, now unfashionable, provides a friendly introduction to the bouncy, red-fruit style of the wine, but for the authentic experience, go for Beaujolais Villages, from the region's better, northern vineyards. There are ten AC zones within this northern sector making wines under their own names. Known as the *crus*, these are Brouilly, Chénas, Chiroubles, Côte de Brouilly, Fleurie, Juliénas, Morgon, Moulin à Vent, Regnié and St Amour. Prices are higher than those for Beaujolais Villages, but not always justifiably so.

Beaumes de Venise – Village near Châteauneuf du Pape in France's Rhône valley, famous for sweet and alcoholic wine from Muscat grapes. Delicious, grapey wines. A small number of growers also make strong (sometimes rather tough) red wines under the village name.

Beaune – One of the two centres (the other is Nuits St Georges) of the Côte d'Or, the winemaking heart of Burgundy in France. Three of the region's humbler appellations take the name of the town: Côtes de Beaune, Côtes de Beaune Villages and Hautes Côtes de Beaune.

berry fruit – Some red wines deliver a burst of flavour in the mouth that corresponds to biting into a newly picked berry – strawberry, blackberry, etc. So a wine described as having berry fruit (by this writer, anyway) has freshness, liveliness and immediate appeal.

bianco – White wine, Italy.

Bical – White grape variety principally of Dão region of northern Portugal. Not usually identified on labels, because most of it goes into inexpensive sparkling wines. Can make still wines of very refreshing crispness.

biodynamics – A cultivation method taking the organic approach several steps further. Biodynamic winemakers plant and tend their vineyards according to a date and time calendar 'in harmony' with the movements of the planets. Some of France's best-known wine estates subscribe, and many more are going that way. It might all sound bonkers, but it's salutary to learn that biodynamics is based on principles first described by the eminent Austrian educationist Rudolph Steiner.

bite – In wine-tasting, the impression on the palate of a wine with plenty of acidity and, often, tannin.

blanc – White wine, France.

blanc de blancs – White wine from white grapes, France. May seem to be stating the obvious, but some white wines (e.g. champagne) are made, partially or entirely, from black grapes.

blanc de noirs – White wine from black grapes, France. Usually sparkling (especially champagne) made from black Pinot Meunier and Pinot Noir grapes, with no Chardonnay or other white varieties.

blanco – White wine, Spain and Portugal.

Blauer Zweigelt – Black grape variety of Austria, making a large proportion of the country's red wines, some of excellent quality.

Bobal – Black grape variety mostly of south-eastern Spain. Thick skin is good for colour and juice contributes acidity to blends.

bodega – In Spain, a wine producer or wine shop.

Bonarda – Black grape variety of northern Italy. Now more widely planted in Argentina, where it makes some well-regarded red wines.

botrytis – Full name, *botrytis cinerea*, is that of a beneficent fungus that can attack ripe grape bunches late in the season, shrivelling the berries to a gruesome-looking mess, which yields concentrated juice of prized sweetness. Cheerfully known as 'noble rot', this fungus is actively encouraged by winemakers in regions as diverse as Sauternes (in Bordeaux), Monbazillac (in Bergerac), the Rhine and Mosel valleys, Hungary's Tokaji region and South Australia to make ambrosial dessert wines.

bouncy – The feel in the mouth of a red wine with young, juicy fruitiness. Good Beaujolais is bouncy, as are many north-west-Italian wines from Barbera and Dolcetto grapes.

Bourgogne Grand Ordinaire – Former AC of Burgundy, France. *See* Coteaux Bourguignons.

Bourgueil – Appellation of Loire Valley, France. Long-lived red wines from Cabernet Franc grapes.

briary – In wine tasting, associated with the flavours of fruit from prickly bushes such as blackberries.

brûlé – Pleasant burnt-toffee taste or smell, as in crème brûlée.

brut – Driest style of sparkling wine. Originally French, for very dry champagnes specially developed for the British market, but now used for sparkling wines from all round the world.

Buzet – Little-seen AC of south-west France overshadowed by Bordeaux but producing some characterful ripe reds.

C

Cabardès – AC for red and rosé wines from area north of Carcassonne, Aude, France. Principally Cabernet Sauvignon and Merlot grapes.

Cabernet Franc – Black grape variety originally of France. It makes the light-bodied and keenly edged red wines of the Loire Valley – such as Chinon and Saumur. And it is much grown in Bordeaux, especially in the appellation of St Emilion. Also now planted in Argentina, Australia and North America. Wines, especially in the Loire, are characterised by a leafy, sappy style and bold fruitiness. Most are best enjoyed young.

Cabernet Sauvignon – Black (or, rather, blue) grape variety now grown in virtually every wine-producing nation. When perfectly ripened, the grapes are smaller than many other varieties and have particularly thick skins.

This means that when pressed, Cabernet grapes have a high proportion of skin to juice – and that makes for wine with lots of colour and tannin. In Bordeaux, the grape's traditional home, the grandest Cabernet-based wines have always been known as *vins de garde* (wines to keep) because they take years, even decades, to evolve as the effect of all that skin extraction preserves the fruit all the way to magnificent maturity. But in today's impatient world, these grapes are exploited in modern winemaking techniques to produce the sublime flavours of mature Cabernet without having to hang around for lengthy periods awaiting maturation. While there's nothing like a fine, ten-year-old claret (and few quite as expensive), there are many excellent Cabernets from around the world that amply illustrate this grape's characteristics. Classic smells and flavours include blackcurrants, cedar wood, chocolate, tobacco – even violets.

Cahors – An AC of the Lot Valley in south-west France once famous for 'black wine'. This was a curious concoction of straightforward wine mixed with a soupy must, made by boiling up new-pressed juice to concentrate it (through evaporation) before fermentation. The myth is still perpetuated that Cahors wine continues to be made in this way, but production on this basis actually ceased 150 years ago. Cahors today is no stronger, or blacker, than the wines of neighbouring appellations. Principal grape variety is Malbec, known locally as Cot.

Cairanne – Village of the appellation collectively known as the Côtes du Rhône in southern France. Cairanne is one of several villages entitled to put their name on the labels of wines made within their AC boundary, and the appearance of this name is quite reliably an indicator of quality.

Calatayud – DO (quality wine zone) near Zaragoza in the Aragon region of northern Spain where they're making some astonishingly good wines at bargain prices, mainly reds from Garnacha and Tempranillo grapes. These are the varieties that go into the polished and oaky wines of Rioja, but in Calatayud, the wines are dark, dense and decidedly different.

Cannonau – Black grape native to Sardinia by name, but in fact the same variety as the ubiquitous Grenache of France (and Garnacha of Spain).

cantina sociale – *See* co-op.

Carignan – Black grape variety of Mediterranean France. It is rarely identified on labels, but is a major constituent of wines from the southern Rhône and Languedoc-Roussillon regions. Known as Carignano in Italy and Cariñena in Spain.

Cariñena – A region of north-east Spain, south of Navarra, known for substantial reds, as well as the Spanish name for the Carignan grape (*qv*).

Carmenère – Black grape variety once widely grown in Bordeaux but abandoned due to cultivation problems. Lately revived in South America where it is producing fine wines, sometimes with echoes of Bordeaux.

cassis – As a tasting note, signifies a wine that has a noticeable blackcurrant-concentrate flavour or smell. Much associated with the Cabernet Sauvignon grape.

Castelao – Portuguese black grape variety. Same as Periquita.

Catarratto – White grape variety of Sicily. In skilled hands it can make anything from keen, green-fruit dry whites to lush, oaked super-ripe styles. Also used for Marsala.

cat's pee – In tasting notes, a jocular reference to the smell of a certain style of Sauvignon Blanc wine.

cava – The sparkling wine of Spain. Most originates in Catalonia, but the Denominación de Origen (DO) guarantee of authenticity is open to producers in many regions of the country. Much cava is very reasonably priced even though it is made by the same method as champagne – second fermentation in bottle, known in Spain as the *método clásico*.

CdR – Côtes du Rhône. My own shorthand.

cépage – Grape variety, French. 'Cépage Merlot' on a label simply means the wine is made largely or exclusively from Merlot grapes.

Chablis – Northernmost AC of France's Burgundy region. Its dry white wines from Chardonnay grapes are known for their fresh and steely style, but the best wines also age very gracefully into complex classics.

Chambourcin – Sounds like a cream cheese but it's a relatively modern (1963) French hybrid black grape that makes some good non-appellation lightweight-but-concentrated reds in the Loire Valley and now some heftier versions in Australia.

champagne – The sparkling wine of the strictly defined Champagne region of France, made by the equally strictly defined champagne method.

Chardonnay – Possibly the world's most popular grape variety. Said to originate from the village of Chardonnay in the Mâconnais region of southern Burgundy, the vine is now planted in every wine-producing nation. Wines are commonly characterised by generous colour and sweet-apple smell, but styles range from lean and sharp to opulently rich. Australia started the craze for oaked Chardonnay, the gold-coloured, super-ripe, buttery 'upfront' wines that are a caricature of lavish and outrageously expensive burgundies such as Meursault and Puligny-Montrachet. Rich to the point of egginess, these Aussie pretenders are now giving way to a sleeker, more minerally style with much less oak presence – if any at all. California and Chile, New Zealand and South Africa are competing hard to imitate the Burgundian style, and Australia's success in doing so.

Châteauneuf du Pape – Famed appellation centred on a picturesque village of the southern Rhône valley in France where in the 1320s French Pope Clement V had a splendid new château built for himself as a summer retreat amidst his vineyards. The red wines of the AC, which can be made from 13 different grape varieties but principally Grenache, Syrah and Mourvèdre, are regarded as the best of the southern Rhône and have become rather expensive – but they can be sensationally good. Expensive white wines are also made.

Chenin Blanc – White grape variety of the Loire Valley, France. Now also grown farther afield, especially in South Africa. Makes dry, soft white wines and also rich, sweet styles.

cherry – In wine tasting, either a pale red colour or, more commonly, a smell or flavour akin to the sun-warmed, bursting sweet ripeness of cherries. Many Italian wines, from lightweights such as Bardolino and Valpolicella to serious Chianti, have this character. 'Black cherry' as a description is often used of Merlot wines – meaning they are sweet but have a firmness of mouthfeel associated with the thicker skins of black cherries.

Cinsault – Black grape variety of southern France, where it is invariably blended with others in wines of all qualities from country reds to pricy appellations such as Châteauneuf du Pape. Also much planted in South Africa. The effect in wine is to add keen aromas (sometimes compared with turpentine) and softness to the blend. The name is often spelt Cinsaut.

Clape, La – A small *cru* (defined quality-vineyard area) within the Coteaux du Languedoc where the growers make some seriously delicious red wines, mainly from Carignan, Grenache and Syrah grapes. A name worth looking out for on labels from the region.

claret – The red wine of Bordeaux, France. Old British nickname from Latin *clarus*, meaning 'clear', recalling a time when the red wines of the region were much lighter in colour than they are now.

clarete – On Spanish labels indicates a pale-coloured red wine. Tinto signifies a deeper hue.

classed growth – English translation of French *cru classé* describes a group of 60 individual wine estates in the Médoc district of Bordeaux, which in 1855 were granted this new status on the basis that their wines were the most expensive of the day. The classification was a promotional wheeze to attract attention to the Bordeaux stand at that year's Great Exhibition in Paris. Amazingly, all of the wines concerned are still in production and most still occupy more or less their original places in the pecking order price-wise. The league was divided up into five divisions from *Premier Grand Cru Classé* (just four wines originally, with one promoted in 1971 – the only change ever made to the classification) to *Cinquième Grand Cru Classé*. Other regions of Bordeaux, notably Graves and St Emilion, have since imitated Médoc and introduced their own rankings of *cru classé* estates.

classic – An overused term in every respect – wine descriptions being no exception. In this book, the word is used to describe a very good wine of its type. So, a 'classic' Cabernet Sauvignon is one that is recognisably and admirably characteristic of that grape.

Classico – Under Italy's wine laws, this word appended to the name of a DOC or DOCG zone has an important significance. The classico wines of the region can only be made from vineyards lying in the best-rated areas, and wines thus labelled (e.g. Chianti Classico, Soave Classico, Valpolicella Classico) can be reliably counted on to be a cut above the rest.

Colombard – White grape variety of southern France. Once employed almost entirely for making the wine that is distilled for armagnac and cognac brandies, but lately restored to varietal prominence in the Côtes de Gascogne where high-tech wineries turn it into a fresh and crisp, if unchallenging, dry wine at a budget price. But beware, cheap Colombard (especially from South Africa) can still be very dull.

Conca de Barbera – Winemaking region of Catalonia, Spain.

co-op – Very many of France's good-quality, inexpensive wines are made by co-operatives. These are wine-producing centres whose members, and joint-owners, are local *vignerons* (vine growers). Each year they sell their harvests to the co-op for turning into branded wines. In Italy, co-op wines can be identified by the words *Cantina Sociale* on the label and in Germany by the term *Winzergenossenschaft*.

Corbières – A name to look out for. It's an AC of France's Midi (deep south) and produces countless robust reds and a few interesting whites, often at bargain prices.

Cortese – White grape variety of Piedmont, Italy. At its best, makes delicious, keenly brisk and fascinating wines, including those of the Gavi DOCG. Worth seeking out.

Costières de Nîmes – Until 1989, this AC of southern France was known as the Costières de Gard. It forms a buffer between the southern Rhône and Languedoc-Roussillon regions, and makes wines from broadly the same range of grape varieties. It's a name to look out for, the best red wines being notable for their concentration of colour and fruit, with the earthy-spiciness of the better Rhône wines and a likeable liquorice note. A few good white wines, too, and even a decent rosé or two.

Côte – In French, it simply means a side, or slope, of a hill. The implication in wine terms is that the grapes come from a vineyard ideally situated for maximum sunlight, good drainage and the unique soil conditions prevailing on the hill in question. It's fair enough to claim that vines grown on slopes might get more sunlight than those grown on the flat, but there is no guarantee whatsoever that any wine labelled 'Côtes du' this or that is made from grapes grown on a hillside anyway. Côtes du Rhône wines are a case in point. Many 'Côtes' wines come from entirely level vineyards and it is worth remembering that many of the vineyards of Bordeaux, producing most of the world's priciest wines, are little short of prairie-flat. The quality factor is determined much more significantly by the weather and the talents of the winemaker.

Coteaux Bourguignons – Generic AC of Burgundy, France, since 2011 for red and rosé wines from Pinot Noir and Gamay grapes, and white wines from (principally) Chardonnay and Bourgogne Aligoté grapes. The AC replaces the former appellation Bourgogne Grand Ordinaire.

Côtes de Blaye – Appellation Contrôlée zone of Bordeaux on the right bank of the River Gironde, opposite the more prestigious Médoc zone of the left bank. Best-rated vineyards qualify for the AC Premières Côtes de Blaye. A couple of centuries ago, Blaye (pronounced 'bligh') was the grander of the two, and even today makes some wines that compete well for quality, and at a fraction of the price of wines from its more fashionable rival across the water.

Côtes de Bourg – AC neighbouring Côtes de Blaye, making red wines of decent quality and value.

Côtes du Luberon – Appellation Contrôlée zone of Provence in south-east France. Wines, mostly red, are similar in style to Côtes du Rhône.

Côtes du Rhône – One of the biggest and best-known appellations of south-east France, covering an area roughly defined by the southern reaches of the valley of the River Rhône. The Côtes du Rhône AC achieves notably consistent quality at all points along the price scale. Lots of brilliant-value warm and spicy reds, principally from Grenache and Syrah grapes. There are also some white and rosé wines.

Côtes du Rhône Villages – Appellation within the larger Côtes du Rhône AC for wine of supposed superiority made in a number of zones associated with a long list of nominated individual villages.

Côtes du Roussillon – Huge appellation of south-west France known for strong, dark, peppery reds often offering very decent value.

Côtes du Roussillon Villages – Appellation for superior wines from a number of nominated locations within the larger Roussillon AC. Some of these village wines can be of exceptional quality and value.

crianza – Means 'nursery' in Spanish. On Rioja and Navarra wines, the designation signifies a wine that has been nursed through a maturing period of at least a year in oak casks and a further six months in bottle before being released for sale.

cru – A word that crops up with confusing regularity on French wine labels. It means 'the growing' or 'the making' of a wine and asserts that the wine concerned is from a specific vineyard. Under the Appellation Contrôlée rules, countless *crus* are classified in various hierarchical ranks. Hundreds of individual vineyards are described as *premier cru* or *grand cru* in the classic wine regions of Alsace, Bordeaux, Burgundy and Champagne. The common denominator is that the wine can be counted on to be expensive. On humbler wines, the use of the word *cru* tends to be mere decoration.

cru classé – *See* classed growth.

cuve – A vat for wine. French.

cuvée – French for the wine in a *cuve*, or vat. The word is much used on labels to imply that the wine is from just one vat, and thus of unique, unblended character. *Première cuvée* is supposedly the best wine from a given pressing because it comes from the free-run juice of grapes crushed by their own weight before pressing begins. Subsequent *cuvées* will have been from harsher pressings, grinding the grape pulp to extract the last drops of juice.

D

Dão – Major wine-producing region of northern Portugal now turning out much more interesting reds than it used to – worth looking out for anything made by mega-producer Sogrape.

demi sec – 'Half-dry' style of French (and some other) wines. Beware. It can mean anything from off-dry to cloyingly sweet.

DO – Denominación de Origen, Spain's wine-regulating scheme, similar to France's AC, but older – the first DO region was Rioja, from 1926. DO wines are Spain's best, accounting for a third of the nation's annual production.

DOC – Stands for Denominazione di Origine Controllata, Italy's equivalent of France's AC. The wines are made according to the stipulations of each of the system's 300-plus denominated zones of origin, along with a further 74 zones, which enjoy the superior classification of DOCG (DOC with *e Garantita* – guaranteed – appended).

DOCa – *Denominación de Origen Calificada* is Spain's highest regional wine classification; currently only Priorat and Rioja qualify.

DOP – Denominazione di Origine Protetta is an alternative classification to DOC (*qv*) under EU directive in Italy, comparable to AOP (*qv*) in France, but not yet widely adopted.

Durif – Rare black grape variety mostly of California, where it is also known as Petite Sirah, with some plantings in Australia.

E

earthy – A tricky word in the wine vocabulary. In this book, its use is meant to be complimentary. It indicates that the wine somehow suggests the soil the grapes were grown in, even (perhaps a shade too poetically) the landscape in which the vineyards lie. The amazing-value red wines of the torrid, volcanic southernmost regions of Italy are often described as earthy. This is an association with the pleasantly 'scorched' back-flavour in wines made from the ultra-ripe harvests of this near-sub-tropical part of the world.

edge – A wine with edge is one with evident (although not excessive) acidity.

élevé – 'Brought up' in French. Much used on wine labels where the wine has been matured (brought up) in oak barrels, *élevé en fûts de chêne*, to give it extra dimensions.

Entre Deux Mers – Meaning 'between two seas', it's a region lying between the Dordogne and Garonne rivers of Bordeaux, now mainly known for dry white wines from Sauvignon Blanc and Semillon grapes.

Estremadura – Wine-producing region occupying Portugal's coastal area north of Lisbon. Lots of interesting wines from indigenous grape varieties, often at bargain prices. If a label mentions Estremadura, it is a safe rule that there might be something good within.

Extremadura – Minor wine-producing region of western Spain abutting the frontier with Portugal's Alentejo region. Not to be confused with Estremadura of Portugal (above).

F

Falanghina – Revived ancient grape variety of southern Italy now making some superbly fresh and tangy white wines.

Faugères – AC of the Languedoc in south-west France. Source of many hearty, economic reds.

Feteasca – White grape variety widely grown in Romania. Name means 'maiden's grape' and the wine tends to be soft and slightly sweet.

Fiano – White grape variety of the Campania of southern Italy and Sicily, lately revived. It is said to have been cultivated by the ancient Romans for a wine called Apianum.

finish – The last flavour lingering in the mouth after wine has been swallowed.

fino – Pale and very dry style of sherry. You drink it thoroughly chilled – and you don't keep it any longer after opening than other dry white wines. Needs to be fresh to be at its best.

Fitou – AC of Languedoc, France. Red wines principally from Carignan, Grenache, Mourvèdre and Syrah grapes.

flabby – Fun word describing a wine that tastes dilute or watery, with insufficient acidity.

Frappato – Black grape variety of Sicily. Light red wines.

fruit – In tasting terms, the fruit is the greater part of the overall flavour of a wine. The wine is, after all, composed entirely of fruit

G

Gamay – The black grape that makes all red Beaujolais and some ordinary burgundy. It is a pretty safe rule to avoid Gamay wines from other regions.

Garganega – White grape variety of the Veneto region of north-east Italy. Best known as the principal ingredient of Soave, but occasionally included in varietal blends and mentioned as such on labels. Correctly pronounced 'gar-GAN-iga'.

Garnacha – Spanish black grape variety synonymous with Grenache of France. It is blended with Tempranillo to make the red wines of Rioja and Navarra, and is now quite widely cultivated elsewhere in Spain to make grippingly fruity varietals.

garrigue – Arid land of France's deep south giving its name to a style of red wine that notionally evokes the herby, heated, peppery flavours associated with such a landscape and its flora. A tricky metaphor.

Gavi – DOCG for dry aromatic white wine from Cortese grapes in Piedmont, north-west Italy. Trendy Gavi di Gavi wines tend to be enjoyably lush, but are rather expensive.

Gewürztraminer – One of the great grape varieties of Alsace, France. At their best, the wines are perfumed with lychees and are richly, spicily fruity, yet quite dry. Gewürztraminer from Alsace can be expensive, but the grape is also grown with some success in Germany, Italy, New Zealand and South America, at more approachable prices. Pronounced 'ge-VOORTS-traminner'.

Givry – AC for red and white wines in the Côte Chalonnaise sub-region of Burgundy. Source of some wonderfully natural-tasting reds that might be lighter than those of the more prestigious Côte d'Or to the north, but have great merits of their own. Relatively, the wines are often underpriced.

Glera – New official name for the Prosecco grape of northern Italy.

Godello – White grape variety of Galicia, Spain.

Graciano – Black grape variety of Spain that is one of the minor constituents of Rioja. Better known in its own right in Australia where it can make dense, spicy, long-lived red wines.

green – I don't often use this in the pejorative. Green, to me, is a likeable degree of freshness, especially in Sauvignon Blanc wines.

Grecanico – White grape variety of southern Italy, especially Sicily. Aromatic, grassy dry white wines.

Greco – White grape variety of southern Italy believed to be of ancient Greek origin. Big-flavoured dry white wines.

Grenache – The mainstay of the wines of the southern Rhône Valley in France. Grenache is usually the greater part of the mix in Côtes du Rhône reds and is widely planted right across the neighbouring Languedoc-Roussillon region. It's a big-cropping variety that thrives even in the hottest climates and is really a blending grape – most commonly with Syrah, the noble variety of the northern Rhône. Few French wines are labelled with its name, but the grape has caught on in Australia in a big way and it is now becoming a familiar varietal, known for strong, dark liquorous reds. Grenache is the French name for what is originally a Spanish variety, Garnacha.

Grillo – White grape of Sicily said to be among the island's oldest indigenous varieties, pre-dating the arrival of the Greeks in 600 BC. Much used for fortified Marsala, it has lately been revived for interesting, aromatic dry table wines.

grip – In wine-tasting terminology, the sensation in the mouth produced by a wine that has a healthy quantity of tannin in it. A wine with grip is a good wine. A wine with too much tannin, or which is still too young (the tannin hasn't 'softened' with age) is not described as having grip, but as mouth-puckering – or simply undrinkable.

Grolleau – Black grape variety of the Loire Valley principally cultivated for Rosé d'Anjou.

Gros Plant – White grape variety of the Pays Nantais in France's Loire estuary; synonymous with the Folle Blanche grape of south-west France.

Grüner Veltliner – The 'national' white-wine grape of Austria. In the past it made mostly soft, German-style everyday wines, but now is behind some excellent dry styles, too.

H

halbtrocken – 'Half-dry' in Germany's wine vocabulary. A reassurance that the wine is not a sugared Liebfraumilch-style confection.

hard – In red wine, a flavour denoting excess tannin, probably due to immaturity.

Haut-Médoc – Extensive AC of Bordeaux accounting for the greater part of the vineyard area to the north of the city of Bordeaux west of the Gironde river. The Haut-Médoc incorporates the prestigious commune-ACs of Listrac, Margaux, Moulis, Pauillac, St Estèphe and St Julien.

Hermitage – AC of northern Rhône Valley, France for red wines from Syrah grapes and some whites. Hermitage is also the regional name in South Africa for the Cinsaut grape.

hock – The wine of Germany's Rhine river valleys. Traditionally, but no longer consistently, it comes in brown bottles, as distinct from the wine of the Mosel river valleys – which comes in green ones.

Hunter Valley – Long-established (1820s) wine-producing region of New South Wales, Australia.

I

Indicación Geográfica Protegida (IGP) – Spain's country-wine quality designation covers 46 zones across the country. Wines made under the IGP can be labelled Vino de la Tierra.

Indication Géographique Protégée (IGP) – Introduced to France in 2010 under EU-wide wine-designation rules, IGP covers the wines previously known as vins de pays. Some wines are currently labelled IGP, but established vins de pays producers are redesignating slowly, if at all, and are not obliged to do so. Some will abbreviate, so, for example, Vin de Pays d'Oc shortens to Pays d'Oc.

Indicazione Geografica Tipica (IGT) – Italian wine-quality designation, broadly equivalent to France's IGP. The label has to state the geographical location of the vineyard and will often (but not always) state the principal grape varieties from which the wine is made.

isinglass – A gelatinous material used in fining (clarifying) wine. It is derived from fish bladders and consequently is eschewed by makers of 'vegetarian' or 'vegan' wines.

J

jammy – The 'sweetness' in dry red wines is supposed to evoke ripeness rather than sugariness. Sometimes, flavours include a sweetness reminiscent of jam. Usually a fault in the winemaking technique.

Jerez – Wine town of Andalucia, Spain, and home to sherry. The English word 'sherry' is a simple mispronunciation of Jerez.

joven – Young wine, Spanish. In regions such as Rioja, *vino joven* is a synonym for *sin crianza*, which means 'without ageing' in cask or bottle.

Jura – Wine region of eastern France incorporating four AOCs, Arbois, Château-Chalon, Côtes du Jura and L'Etoile. Known for still red, white and rosé wines and sparkling wines as well as exotic *vin de paille* and *vin jaune.*

Jurançon – Appellation for white wines from Courbu and Manseng grapes at Pau, south-west France.

K

Kabinett – Under Germany's bewildering wine-quality rules, this is a classification of a top-quality (QmP) wine. Expect a keen, dry, racy style. The name comes from the cabinet or cupboard in which winemakers traditionally kept their most treasured bottles.

Kekfrankos – Black grape variety of Hungary, particularly the Sopron region, which makes some of the country's more interesting red wines, characterised by colour and spiciness. Same variety as Austria's Blaufrankisch.

L

Ladoix – Unfashionable AC at northern edge of Côtes de Beaune makes some of Burgundy's true bargain reds. A name to look out for.

Lambrusco – The name is that of a black grape variety widely grown across northern Italy. True Lambrusco wine is red, dry and very slightly sparkling, and enjoying a current vogue in Britain.

Languedoc-Roussillon – Extensive wine region of southern France incorporating numerous ACs and IGP zones, notably the Pays d'Oc and Côtes de Roussillon.

lees – The detritus of the winemaking process that collects in the bottom of the vat or cask. Wines left for extended periods on the lees can acquire extra dimensions of flavour, in particular a 'leesy' creaminess.

legs – The liquid residue left clinging to the sides of the glass after wine has been swirled. The persistence of the legs is an indicator of the weight of alcohol. Also known as 'tears'.

lieu dit – This is starting to appear on French wine labels. It translates as an 'agreed place' and is an area of vineyard defined as of particular character or merit, but not classified under wine law. Usually, the *lieu dit*'s name is stated, with the implication that the wine in question has special merit.

liquorice – The pungent, slightly burnt flavours of this confection are detectable in some wines made from very ripe grapes, for example, the Malbec harvested in Argentina and several varieties grown in the very hot vineyards of southernmost Italy. A close synonym is 'tarry'. This characteristic is by no means a fault in red wine, unless very dominant, but it can make for a challenging flavour that might not appeal to all tastes.

liquorous – Wines of great weight and glyceriney texture (evidenced by the 'legs', or 'tears', which cling to the glass after the wine has been swirled) are always noteworthy. The connection with liquor is drawn in respect of the feel of the wine in the mouth, rather than with the higher alcoholic strength of spirits.

Lirac – Village and AC of southern Rhône Valley, France. A near-neighbour of the esteemed appellation of Châteauneuf du Pape, Lirac makes red wine of comparable depth and complexity, at competitive prices.

Lugana – DOC of Lombardy, Italy, known for a dry white wine that is often of real distinction – rich, almondy stuff from the ubiquitous Trebbiano grape.

M

Macabeo – One of the main grapes used for cava, the sparkling wine of Spain. It is the same grape as Viura.

Mâcon – Town and collective appellation of southern Burgundy, France. Minerally white wines from Chardonnay grapes and light reds from Pinot Noir and some Gamay. The better ones, and the ones exported, have the AC Mâcon-Villages and there are individual village wines with their own ACs including Mâcon-Clessé, Mâcon-Viré and Mâcon-Lugny.

Malbec – Black grape variety grown on a small scale in Bordeaux, and the mainstay of the wines of Cahors in France's Dordogne region under the name Cot. Now much better known for producing big butch reds in Argentina.

malolactic fermentation – In winemaking, a common natural bacterial action following alcoholic fermentation, converting malic (apple) acid into lactic (milk) acid. The effect is to reduce tartness and to boost creaminess in the wine. Adding lactic bacteria to wine to promote the process is widely practised.

manzanilla – Pale, very dry sherry of Sanlucar de Barrameda, a resort town on the Bay of Cadiz in Spain. Manzanilla is proud to be distinct from the pale, very dry fino sherry of the main producing town of Jerez de la Frontera an hour's drive inland. Drink it chilled and fresh – it goes downhill in an opened bottle after just a few days, even if kept (as it should be) in the fridge.

Margaret River – Vineyard region of Western Australia regarded as ideal for grape varieties including Cabernet Sauvignon. It has a relatively cool climate and a reputation for making sophisticated wines, both red and white.

Marlborough – Best-known vineyard region of New Zealand's South Island has a cool climate and a name for brisk but cerebral Sauvignon Blanc and Chardonnay wines.

Marsanne – White grape variety of the northern Rhône Valley and, increasingly, of the wider south of France. It's known for making well-coloured wines with heady aroma and nuanced fruit.

Mataro – Black grape variety of Australia. It's the same as the Mourvèdre of France and Monastrell of Spain.

Mazuelo – Spanish name for France's black grape variety Carignan.

McLaren Vale – Vineyard region south of Adelaide in south-east Australia. Known for blockbuster Shiraz (and Chardonnay) that can be of great balance and quality from winemakers who manage to keep the ripeness under control.

meaty – In wine-tasting, a weighty, rich red wine style.

Mencia – Black grape variety of Galicia and north-west Spain. Light red wines.

Mendoza – Wine region of Argentina. Lying to the east of the Andes mountains, just about opposite the best vineyards of Chile on the other side, Mendoza accounts for the bulk of Argentine wine production.

Merlot – One of the great black wine grapes of Bordeaux, and now grown all over the world. The name is said to derive from the French *merle*, a blackbird. Characteristics of Merlot-based wines attract descriptions such as 'plummy' and 'plump' with black-cherry aromas. The grapes are larger than most, and thus have less skin in proportion to their flesh. This means the resulting wines have less tannin than wines from smaller-berry varieties such as Cabernet Sauvignon, and are therefore, in the Bordeaux context at least, more suitable for drinking while still relatively young.

middle palate – In wine-tasting, the impression given by the wine after the first impact on 'entry' and before the 'finish' when the wine is swallowed.

Midi – Catch-all term for the deep south of France west of the Rhône Valley.

mineral – Irresistible term in wine-tasting. To me it evokes flavours such as the stone-pure freshness of some Loire dry whites, or the flinty quality of the more austere style of the Chardonnay grape, especially in Chablis. Mineral really just means something mined, as in dug out of the ground, like iron ore (as in 'steely' whites) or rock, as in, er, stone. Maybe there's something in it, but I am not entirely confident.

Minervois – AC for (mostly) red wines from vineyards around the Roman-founded town of Minerve in the Languedoc-Roussillon region of France. Often good value. The recently elevated Minervois La Livinière AC is a sort of Minervois *grand cru*.

Monastrell – Black grape variety of Spain, widely planted in Mediterranean regions for inexpensive wines notable for their high alcohol and toughness – though they can mature into excellent, soft reds. The variety is known in France as Mourvèdre and in Australia as Mataro.

Monbazillac – AC for sweet, dessert wines within the wider appellation of Bergerac in south-west France. Made from the same grape varieties (principally Sauvignon and Semillon) that go into the much costlier counterpart wines of Barsac and Sauternes near Bordeaux, these stickies from botrytis-affected, late-harvested grapes can be delicious and good value for money.

Montalcino – Hill town of Tuscany, Italy, and a DOCG for strong and very long-lived red wines from Brunello grapes. The wines are mostly very expensive. Rosso di Montalcino, a DOC for the humbler wines of the zone, is often a good buy.

Montepulciano – Black grape variety of Italy. Best known in Montepulciano d'Abruzzo, the juicy, purply-black and bramble-fruited red of the Abruzzi region midway down Italy's Adriatic side. Also the grape in the rightly popular hearty reds of Rosso Conero from around Ancona in the Marches. Not to be confused with the hill town of Montepulciano in Tuscany, famous for expensive Vino Nobile di Montepulciano wine, made from Sangiovese grapes.

morello – Lots of red wines have smells and flavours redolent of cherries. Morello cherries, among the darkest coloured and sweetest of all varieties and the preferred choice of cherry-brandy producers, have a distinct sweetness resembled by some wines made from Merlot grapes. A morello whiff or taste is generally very welcome.

Moscatel – Spanish Muscat.

Moscato – *See* Muscat.

moselle – The wine of Germany's Mosel river valleys, collectively known for winemaking purposes as the Mosel-Saar-Ruwer. The wine always comes in slim, green bottles, as distinct from the brown bottles traditionally, but no longer exclusively, employed for Rhine wines.

Mourvèdre – Widely planted black grape variety of southern France. It's an ingredient in many of the wines of Provence, the Rhône and Languedoc, including the ubiquitous Pays d'Oc. It's a hot-climate vine and the wine is usually blended with other varieties to give sweet aromas and 'backbone' to the mix. Known as Mataro in Australia and Monastrell in Spain.

Muscadet – One of France's most familiar everyday whites, made from a grape called the Melon or Melon de Bourgogne. It comes from vineyards at the estuarial end of the River Loire, and has a sea-breezy freshness about it. The better wines are reckoned to be those from the vineyards in the Sèvre et Maine region, and many are made *sur lie* – 'on the lees' – meaning that the wine is left in contact with the yeasty deposit of its fermentation until just before bottling, in an endeavour to add interest to what can sometimes be an acidic and fruitless style.

Muscat – Grape variety with origins in ancient Greece, and still grown widely among the Aegean islands for the production of sweet white wines. Muscats are the wines that taste more like grape juice than any other – but the high sugar levels ensure they are also among the most alcoholic of wines, too. Known as Moscato in Italy, the grape is much used for making sweet sparkling wines, as in Asti Spumante or Moscato d'Asti. There are several appellations in south-west France for inexpensive Muscats made rather like port, part-fermented before the addition of grape alcohol to halt the conversion of sugar into alcohol, creating a sweet and heady *vin doux naturel*. Dry Muscat wines, when well made, have a delicious sweet aroma but a refreshing, light touch with flavours reminiscent variously of orange blossom, wood smoke and grapefruit.

must – New-pressed grape juice prior to fermentation.

N

Navarra – DO wine-producing region of northern Spain adjacent to, and overshadowed by, Rioja. Navarra's wines can be startlingly akin to their neighbouring rivals, and sometimes rather better value for money.

négociant – In France, a dealer-producer who buys wines from growers and matures and/or blends them for bottling and sale under his or her own label. Purists can be a bit sniffy about these entrepreneurs, claiming that only the vine-grower with his or her own winemaking set-up can make truly authentic stuff, but the truth is that many of the best wines of France are *négociant*-produced – especially at the humbler end of the price scale. *Négociants* are often identified on wine labels as *négociant-éleveur* (literally 'dealer-bringer-up'), meaning that the wine has been matured, blended and bottled by the party in question.

Negroamaro – Black grape variety mainly of Puglia, the much-lauded wine region of south-east Italy. Dense, earthy red wines with ageing potential and plenty of alcohol. The name is probably (if not obviously) derived from Italian *negro* (black) and *amaro* (bitter). The grape behind Copertino, Salice Salentino and Squinzano.

Nerello Mascalese – Black grape of Sicily, most prolific in vineyards surrounding Mount Etna, making distinctive, flavoursome reds.

Nero d'Avola – Black grape variety of Sicily (Avola is a town in the province of Syracuse) and southern Italy. It makes deep-coloured wines that, given half a chance, can develop intensity and richness with age.

non-vintage – A wine is described as such when it has been blended from the harvests of more than one year. A non-vintage wine is not necessarily an inferior one, but under quality-control regulations around the world, still table wines most usually derive solely from one year's grape crop to qualify for appellation status. Champagnes and sparkling wines are mostly blended from several vintages, as are fortified wines such as port and sherry.

nose – In the vocabulary of the wine-taster, the nose is the scent of a wine. Sounds a bit dotty, but it makes a sensible enough alternative to the rather bald 'smell'. The use of the word 'perfume' implies that the wine smells particularly good. 'Aroma' is used specifically to describe a wine that smells as it should, as in 'this burgundy has the authentic strawberry-raspberry aroma of Pinot Noir'.

O

oak – Most of the world's costliest wines are matured in new or nearly new oak barrels, giving additional opulence of flavour. Of late, many cheaper wines have been getting the oak treatment, too, in older, cheaper casks, or simply by having sacks of oak chippings poured into their steel or fibreglass holding tanks. 'Oak aged' on a label is likely to indicate the latter treatments. But the overtly oaked wines of Australia have in some cases been so overdone that there is now a reactive trend whereby some producers proclaim their wines – particularly Chardonnays – as 'unoaked' on the label, thereby asserting that the flavours are more naturally achieved.

Oltrepo Pavese – Wine-producing zone of Piedmont, north-west Italy. The name means 'south of Pavia across the [river] Po' and the wines, both white and red, can be excellent quality and value for money.

organic wine – As in other sectors of the food industry, demand for organically made wine is – or appears to be – growing. As a rule, a wine qualifies as organic if it comes entirely from grapes grown in vineyards cultivated without the use of synthetic materials, and made in a winery where chemical treatments or additives are shunned with similar vigour. In fact, there are plenty of winemakers in the world using organic methods, but who disdain to label their bottles as such. Wines proclaiming their organic status used to carry the same sort of premium as their counterparts round the corner in the fruit, vegetable and meat aisles. But organic viticulture is now commonplace and there seems little price impact. There is no single worldwide (or even Europe-wide) standard for organic food or wine, so you pretty much have to take the producer's word for it.

P

Pasqua – One of the biggest and, it should be said, best wine producers of the Veneto region of north-west Italy.

Passerina – White grape variety of Marche, Italy. Used in blending but there is also a regional Passerina DOC.

Passetoutgrains – Designation for wine made from more than one grape variety grown in the same vineyard. French. Mostly red burgundy from Gamay and Pinot Noir.

Pays d'Oc – Shortened form under recent rule changes of French wine designation Vin de Pays d'Oc. All other similar regional designations can be similarly abbreviated.

Pecorino – White grape variety of mid-eastern Italy currently in vogue for well-coloured dry white varietal wines.

Periquita – Black grape variety of southern Portugal. Makes rather exotic spicy reds. Name means 'parrot'.

Perricone – Black grape variety of Sicily. Low-acid red wines.

PET – It's what they call plastic wine bottles – lighter to transport and allegedly as ecological as glass. Polyethylene terephthalate.

Petit Verdot – Black grape variety of Bordeaux contributing additional colour, density and spiciness to Cabernet Sauvignon-dominated blends. Mostly a minority player at home, but in Australia and California it is grown as the principal variety for some big hearty reds of real character.

petrol – When white wines from certain grapes, especially Riesling, are allowed to age in the bottle for longer than a year or two, they can take on a spirity aroma reminiscent of petrol or diesel. In grand mature German wines, this is considered a good thing.

Picpoul – Grape variety of southern France. Best known in Picpoul de Pinet, a dry white from near Sète on the Golfe de Lyon, lately elevated to AOP status. The name Picpoul (also Piquepoul) means 'stings the lips' – referring to the natural high acidity of the juice.

Piemonte – North-western province of Italy, which we call Piedmont, known for the spumante wines of the town of Asti, plus expensive Barbaresco and Barolo and better-value varietal red wines from Nebbiolo, Barbera and Dolcetto grapes.

Pinotage – South Africa's own black grape variety. Makes red wines ranging from light and juicy to dark, strong and long-lived. It's a cross between Pinot Noir and a grape the South Africans used to call Hermitage (thus the portmanteau name) but turns out to have been Cinsault.

Pinot Blanc – White grape variety principally of Alsace, France. Florally perfumed, exotically fruity dry white wines.

Pinot Grigio – White grape variety of northern Italy. Wines bearing its name are perplexingly fashionable. Good examples have an interesting smoky-pungent aroma and keen, slaking fruit. But most are dull. Originally French, it is at its best in the lushly exotic Pinot Gris wines of Alsace and is also successfully cultivated in Germany and New Zealand.

Pinot Noir – The great black grape of Burgundy, France. It makes all the region's fabulously expensive red wines. Notoriously difficult to grow in warmer climates, it is nevertheless cultivated by countless intrepid winemakers in the New World intent on reproducing the magic appeal of red burgundy. California and New Zealand have come closest. Some Chilean Pinot Noirs are inexpensive and worth trying.

Pouilly Fuissé – Village and AC of the Mâconnais region of southern Burgundy in France. Dry white wines from Chardonnay grapes. Wines are among the highest rated of the Mâconnais.

Pouilly Fumé – Village and AC of the Loire Valley in France. Dry white wines from Sauvignon Blanc grapes. Similar 'pebbly', 'grassy' or 'gooseberry' style to neighbouring AC Sancerre. The notion put about by some enthusiasts that Pouilly Fumé is 'smoky' is surely nothing more than word association with the name.

Primitivo – Black grape variety of southern Italy, especially the region of Puglia. Named from Latin *primus* for first, the grape is among the earliest-ripening of all varieties. The wines are typically dense and dark in colour with plenty of alcohol, and have an earthy, spicy style.

Priorat – Emerging wine region of Catalonia, Spain. Highly valued red wines from Garnacha and other varieties. Generic brands available in supermarkets are well worth trying out.

Prosecco – Softly sparkling wine of Italy's Veneto region. The best come from the DOCG Conegliano-Valdobbiadene, made as spumante ('foaming') wines in pressurised tanks, typically to 11 per cent alcohol and ranging from softly sweet to crisply dry. The constituent grape, previously also known as Prosecco, has been officially assigned the name Glera.

Puglia – The region occupying the 'heel' of southern Italy, making many good, inexpensive wines from indigenous grape varieties.

Q

QbA – German, standing for Qualitätswein bestimmter Anbaugebiete. It means 'quality wine from designated areas' and implies that the wine is made from grapes with a minimum level of ripeness, but it's by no means a guarantee of exciting quality. Only wines labelled QmP (see next entry) can be depended upon to be special.

QmP – Stands for Qualitätswein mit Prädikat. These are the serious wines of Germany, made without the addition of sugar to 'improve' them. To qualify for QmP status, the grapes must reach a level of ripeness as measured on a sweetness scale – all according to Germany's fiendishly complicated wine-quality regulations. Wines from grapes that reach the stated minimum level of sweetness qualify for the description of Kabinett. The next level up earns the rank of Spätlese, meaning 'late-picked'. Kabinett wines can be expected to be dry and brisk in style, and Spätlese wines a little bit riper and fuller. The next grade up, Auslese, meaning 'selected harvest', indicates a wine made from super-ripe grapes; it will be golden in colour and honeyed in flavour. A generation ago, these wines were as valued, and as expensive, as any of the world's grandest appellations. Beerenauslese and Trockenbeerenauslese are speciality wines made from individually picked late-harvest grapes.

Quincy – AC of Loire Valley, France, known for pebbly-dry white wines from Sauvignon grapes. The wines are forever compared to those of nearby and much better-known Sancerre – and Quincy often represents better value for money. Pronounced 'KAN-see'.

Quinta – Portuguese for farm or estate. It precedes the names of many of Portugal's best-known wines. It is pronounced 'KEEN-ta'.

R

racy – Evocative wine-tasting description for wine that thrills the tastebuds with a rush of exciting sensations. Good Rieslings often qualify.

raisiny – Wines from grapes that have been very ripe or overripe at harvest can take on a smell and flavour akin to the concentrated, heat-dried sweetness of raisins. As a minor element in the character of a wine, this can add to the appeal but as a dominant characteristic it is a fault.

rancio – Spanish term harking back to Roman times when wines were commonly stored in jars outside, exposed to the sun, so they oxidised and took on a burnt sort of flavour. Today, *rancio* describes a baked – and by no means unpleasant – flavour in fortified wines, particularly sherry and Madeira.

Reserva – In Portugal and Spain, this has genuine significance. The Portuguese use it for special wines with a higher alcohol level and longer ageing, although the precise periods vary between regions. In Spain, especially in the Navarra and Rioja regions, it means the wine must have had at least a year in oak and two in bottle before release.

reserve – On French (as *réserve*) or other wines, this implies special-quality, longer-aged wines, but has no official significance.

residual sugar – There is sugar in all wine, left over from the fermentation process. Some producers now mention the quantity of residual sugar on back labels in grams per litre of wine, even though so far there is no legal obligation to do so. Dry wines, red or white, typically have 3 g/l or fewer.

Above that, you might well be able to taste the sweetness. In southern hemisphere wines, made from grapes that have ripened under more-intense sunlight than their European counterparts, sugar levels can be correspondingly higher. Sweet wines such as Sauternes contain up to 150 g/l. Dry ('brut') sparkling wines made by the 'champagne' method typically have 10 g/l and tank-method fizzes such as prosecco up to 15 g/l.

Retsina – The universal white wine of Greece. It has been traditionally made in Attica, the region of Athens, for a very long time, and is said to owe its origins and name to the ancient custom of sealing amphorae (terracotta jars) of the wine with a gum made from pine resin. Some of the flavour of the resin inevitably transmitted itself into the wine, and ancient Greeks acquired a lasting taste for it.

Reuilly – AC of Loire Valley, France, for crisp dry whites from Sauvignon grapes. Pronounced 'RER-yee'.

Ribatejo – Emerging wine region of Portugal. Worth seeking out on labels of red wines in particular, because new winemakers are producing lively stuff from distinctive indigenous grapes such as Castelao and Trincadeira.

Ribera del Duero – Classic wine region of north-west Spain lying along the River Duero (which crosses the border to become Portugal's Douro, forming the valley where port comes from). It is home to an estate oddly named Vega Sicilia, where red wines of epic quality are made and sold at equally epic prices. Further down the scale, some very good reds are made, too.

Riesling – The noble grape variety of Germany. It is correctly pronounced 'REEZ-ling', not 'RICE-ling'. Once notorious as the grape behind all those boring 'medium' Liebfraumilches and Niersteiners, this grape has had a bad press. In fact, there has never been much, if any, Riesling in German plonk. But the country's best wines, the so-called Qualitätswein mit Prädikat grades, are made almost exclusively with Riesling. These wines range from crisply fresh and appley styles to extravagantly fruity, honeyed wines from late-harvested grapes. Excellent Riesling wines are also made in Alsace and now in Australasia.

Rioja – The principal fine-wine region of Spain, in the country's north east. The pricier wines are noted for their vanilla-pod richness from long ageing in oak casks. Tempranillo and Garnacha grapes make the reds, Viura the whites.

Ripasso – A particular style of Valpolicella wine. New wine is partially refermented in vats that have been used to make Recioto reds (wines made from semi-dried grapes), thus creating a bigger, smoother version of usually light and pale Valpolicella.

Riserva – In Italy, a wine made only in the best vintages, and allowed longer ageing in cask and bottle.

Rivaner – Alternative name for Germany's Müller-Thurgau grape.

Riverland – Vineyard region to the immediate north of the Barossa Valley of South Australia, extending east into New South Wales.

Roditis – White grape variety of Greece, known for fresh dry whites with decent acidity, often included in retsina.

rosso – Red wine, Italy.

Rosso Conero – DOC red wine made in the environs of Ancona in the Marches, Italy. Made from the Montepulciano grape, the wine can provide excellent value for money.

Ruby Cabernet – Black grape variety of California, created by crossing Cabernet Sauvignon and Carignan. Makes soft and squelchy red wine at home and in South Africa.

Rueda – DO of north-west Spain making first-class refreshing dry whites from the indigenous Verdejo grape, imported Sauvignon, and others. Exciting quality, and prices are keen.

Rully – AC of Chalonnais region of southern Burgundy, France. White wines from Chardonnay and red wines from Pinot Noir grapes. Both can be very good and substantially cheaper than their more northerly Burgundian neighbours. Pronounced 'ROO-yee'.

S

Sagrantino – Black grape variety native to Perugia, Italy. Dark, tannic wines best known in DOCG Sagrantino de Montefalco. Now also cultivated in Australia.

Saint Emilion – AC of Bordeaux, France. Centred on the romantic hill town of St Emilion, this famous sub-region makes some of the grandest red wines of France, but also some of the best-value ones. Less fashionable than the Médoc region on the opposite (west) bank of the River Gironde that bisects Bordeaux, St Emilion wines are made largely with the Merlot grape, and are relatively quick to mature. The top wines are classified *1er grand cru classé* and are madly expensive, but many more are classified respectively *grand cru classé* and *grand cru*, and these designations can be seen as a fairly trustworthy indicator of quality. There are several 'satellite' St Emilion ACs named after the villages at their centres, notably Lussac St Emilion, Montagne St Emilion and Puisseguin St Emilion. Some excellent wines are made by estates within these ACs, and at relatively affordable prices thanks to the comparatively humble status of their satellite designations.

Salento – Up-and-coming wine region of southern Italy. Many good bargain reds from local grapes including Nero d'Avola and Primitivo.

Sancerre – AC of the Loire Valley, France, renowned for flinty-fresh Sauvignon Blanc whites and rarer Pinot Noir reds and rosés.

Sangiovese – The local black grape of Tuscany, Italy, is the principal variety used for Chianti. Also planted further south in Italy and in the New World.

Generic Sangiovese di Toscana can make a consoling substitute for costly Chianti.

Saumur – Town and appellation of Loire Valley, France. Characterful minerally red wines from Cabernet Franc grapes, and some whites. Sparkling wines from Chenin Blanc grapes can be good value.

Saumur-Champigny – Separate appellation for red wines from Cabernet Franc grapes of Saumur in the Loire, sometimes very good and lively.

Sauvignon Blanc – French white grape variety now grown worldwide. New Zealand has raised worldwide production values challenging the long supremacy of French ACs in Bordeaux and the Loire Valley. Chile and South Africa aspire similarly. The wines are characterised by aromas of gooseberry, peapod, fresh-cut grass, even asparagus. Flavours are often described as 'grassy' or 'nettly'.

sec – Dry wine style. French.

secco – Dry wine style. Italian.

seco – Dry wine style. Spanish.

Semillon – White grape variety originally of Bordeaux, where it is blended with Sauvignon Blanc to make fresh dry whites and, when harvested very late in the season, the ambrosial sweet whites of Barsac, Sauternes and other appellations. Even in the driest wines, the grape can be recognised from its honeyed, sweet-pineapple, even banana-like aromas. Now widely planted in Australia and Latin America, and frequently blended with Chardonnay to make dry whites, some of them interesting.

sherry – The great aperitif wine of Spain, centred on the Andalusian city of Jerez (the name 'sherry' is an English mispronunciation). There is a lot of sherry-style wine in the world, but only the authentic wine from Jerez and the neighbouring producing centres of Puerta de Santa Maria and Sanlucar de Barrameda may label their wines as such. The Spanish drink real sherry – very dry and fresh, pale in colour and served well-chilled – called fino and manzanilla, and darker but naturally dry variations called amontillado, palo cortado and oloroso.

Shiraz – Australian name for the Syrah grape. The variety is the most widely planted of any in Australia, and makes red wines of wildly varying quality, characterised by dense colour, high alcohol, spicy fruit and generous, cushiony texture.

Somontano – Wine region of north-east Spain. Name means 'under the mountains' – in this case the Pyrenees – and the region has had DO status since 1984. Much innovative winemaking here, with New World styles emerging. Some very good buys. A region to watch.

souple – French wine-tasting term that translates into English as 'supple' or even 'docile' as in 'pliable', but I understand it in the vinous context to mean muscular but soft – a wine with tannin as well as soft fruit.

Spätlese – *See* QmP.

spirity – Some wines, mostly from the New World, are made from grapes so ripe at harvest that their high alcohol content can be detected through a mildly burning sensation on the tongue, similar to the effect of sipping a spirit. Young Port wines can be detectably spirity.

spritzy – Describes a wine with a gentle sparkle. Some young wines are intended to have this elusive fizziness; in others it is a fault.

spumante – Sparkling wine of Italy. Asti Spumante is the best known, from the town of Asti in the north-west Italian province of Piemonte. Many Prosecco wines are labelled as Spumante in style. The term describes wines that are fully sparkling. Frizzante wines have a less vigorous mousse.

stalky – A useful tasting term to describe red wines with flavours that make you think the stalks from the grape bunches must have been fermented along with the must (juice). Red Loire wines and youthful claret very often have this mild astringency. In moderation it's fine, but if it dominates it probably signifies the wine is at best immature and at worst badly made.

Stellenbosch – Town and region at the heart of South Africa's wine industry. It's an hour's drive from Cape Town and the source of much of the country's cheaper wine. Some serious-quality estate wines as well.

stony – Wine-tasting term for keenly dry white wines. It's meant to indicate a wine of purity and real quality, with just the right match of fruit and acidity.

structured – Good wines are not one-dimensional, they have layers of flavour and texture. A structured wine has phases of enjoyment: the 'attack', or first impression in the mouth; the middle palate as the wine is held in the mouth; and the lingering aftertaste.

sugar – *See* residual sugar.

sulphites – Nearly all wines, barring some esoteric 'natural' types of a kind not found in supermarkets are made with the aid of preparations containing sulphur to combat diseases in the vineyards and bacterial infections in the winery. It's difficult to make wine without sulphur. Even 'organic' wines need it. Because some people are sensitive to the traces of sulphur in some wines, worldwide health authorities insist wine labels bear the warning 'Contains sulphites'.

summer fruit – Wine-tasting term intended to convey a smell or taste of soft fruits such as strawberries and raspberries – without having to commit too specifically to which.

superiore – On labels of Italian wines, this is more than an idle boast. Under DOC(G) rules, wines must qualify for the *superiore* designation by reaching one or more specified quality levels, usually a higher alcohol content or an additional period of maturation. Frascati, for example, qualifies for DOC status at 11.5 per cent alcohol, but to be classified *superiore* must have 12 per cent alcohol.

sur lie – Literally, 'on the lees'. It's a term now widely used on the labels of Muscadet wines, signifying that after fermentation has died down, the new wine has been left in the tank over the winter on the lees – the detritus of yeasts and other interesting compounds left over from the turbid fermentation process. The idea is that additional interest is imparted into the flavour of the wine.

Syrah – The noble grape of the Rhône Valley, France. Makes very dark, dense wine characterised by peppery, tarry aromas. Now planted all over southern France and farther afield. In Australia it is known as Shiraz.

T

table wine – Wine that is unfortified and of an alcoholic strength, for UK tax purposes anyway, of no more than 15 per cent. I use the term to distinguish, for example, between the red table wines of the Douro Valley in Portugal and the region's better-known fortified wine, port.

Tafelwein – Table wine, German. The humblest quality designation, which doesn't usually bode very well.

tank method – Bulk-production process for sparkling wines. Base wine undergoes secondary fermentation in a large, sealed vat rather than in individual closed bottles. Also known as the Charmat method after the name of the inventor of the process. Prosecco is made by the tank method.

Tai – White grape variety of north-east Italy, a relative of Sauvignon Blanc. Also known in Italy as Tocai Friulano or, more correctly, Friulano.

Tannat – Black grape of south-west France, notably for wines of Madiran, and lately named as the variety most beneficial to health thanks to its outstanding antioxidant content.

tannin – Well known as the film-forming, teeth-coating component in tea, tannin is a natural compound that occurs in black grape skins and acts as a natural preservative in wine. Its noticeable presence in wine is regarded as a good thing. It gives young everyday reds their dryness, firmness of flavour and backbone. And it helps high-quality reds to retain their lively fruitiness for many years. A grand Bordeaux red when first made, for example, will have purply-sweet, rich fruit and mouth-puckering tannin, but after ten years or so this will have evolved into a delectably fruity, mature wine in which the formerly parching effects of the tannin have receded almost completely, leaving the shade of 'residual tannin' that marks out a great wine approaching maturity.

Tarrango – Black grape variety of Australia.

tarry – On the whole, winemakers don't like critics to say their wines evoke the redolence of road repairs, but I can't help using this term to describe the agreeable, sweet, 'burnt' flavour that is often found at the centre of the fruit in red wines from Argentina, Italy, Portugal and South Africa in particular.

TCA – Dreaded ailment in wine, usually blamed on faulty corks. It stands for 246 *trichloroanisol* and is characterised by a horrible musty smell and flavour in the affected wine. Thanks to technological advances made by cork manufacturers in Portugal – the leading cork nation – TCA is now in retreat.

tears – The colourless alcohol in the wine left clinging to the inside of the glass after the contents have been swirled. Persistent tears (also known as 'legs') indicate a wine of good concentration.

Tempranillo – The great black grape of Spain. Along with Garnacha (Grenache in France) it makes most red Rioja and Navarra wines and, under many pseudonyms, is an important or exclusive contributor to the wines of many other regions of Spain. It is also widely cultivated in South America.

Teroldego – Black grape variety of Trentino, northern Italy. Often known as Teroldego Rotaliano after the Rotaliano region where most of the vineyards lie. Deep-coloured, assertive, green-edged red wines.

terroir – French word for 'ground' or 'soil' has mystical meaning in vineyard country. Winemakers attribute the distinct characteristics of their products, not just to the soil conditions but to the lie of the land and the prevailing (micro)climate, all within the realm of terroir. The word now frequently appears on effusive back labels asserting the unique appeal of the wine. Some critics scoff that terroir is all imagined nonsense.

tinto – On Spanish labels indicates a deeply coloured red wine. Clarete denotes a paler colour. Also Portuguese.

Toro – Quality wine region east of Zamora, Spain.

Torrontes – White grape variety of Argentina. Makes soft, dry wines often with delicious grapey-spicy aroma, similar in style to the classic dry Muscat wines of Alsace, but at more accessible prices.

Touraine – Region encompassing a swathe of the Loire Valley, France. Non-AC wines may be labelled 'Sauvignon de Touraine'.

Touriga Nacional – The most valued black grape variety of the Douro Valley in Portugal, where port is made. The name Touriga now appears on an increasing number of table wines made as sidelines by the port producers. They can be very good, with the same spirity aroma and sleek flavours of port itself, minus the fortification.

Traminer – Grape variety, the same as Gewürztraminer.

Trebbiano – The workhorse white grape of Italy. A productive variety that is easy to cultivate, it seems to be included in just about every ordinary white wine of the entire nation – including Frascati, Orvieto and Soave. It is the same grape as France's Ugni Blanc. There are, however, distinct regional variations of the grape. Trebbiano di Lugana (also known as Turbiana) makes a distinctive white in the DOC of the name, sometimes very good, while Trebbiano di Toscana makes a major contribution to the distinctly less interesting dry whites of Chianti country.

Trincadeira Preta – Portuguese black grape variety native to the port-producing vineyards of the Douro Valley (where it goes under the name Tinta Amarella). In southern Portugal, it produces dark and sturdy table wines.

trocken – 'Dry' German wine. The description does have a particular meaning under German wine law, namely that there is only a low level of unfermented sugar lingering in the wine (9 grams per litre, if you need to know), and this can leave the wine tasting rather austere.

U

Ugni Blanc – The most widely cultivated white grape variety of France and the mainstay of many a cheap dry white wine. To date it has been better known as the provider of base wine for distilling into armagnac and cognac, but lately the name has been appearing on wine labels. Technology seems to be improving the performance of the grape. The curious name is pronounced 'OON-yee', and is the same variety as Italy's ubiquitous Trebbiano.

Utiel-Requena – Region and *Denominación de Origen* of Mediterranean Spain inland from Valencia. Principally red wines from Bobal, Garnacha and Tempranillo grapes grown at relatively high altitude, between 600 and 900 metres.

V

Vacqueyras – Village of the southern Rhône Valley of France in the region better known for its generic appellation, the Côtes du Rhône. Vacqueyras can date its winemaking history all the way back to 1414, but has only been producing under its own village AC since 1991. The wines, from Grenache and Syrah grapes, can be wonderfully silky and intense, spicy and long-lived.

Valdepeñas – An island of quality production amidst the ocean of mediocrity that is Spain's La Mancha region – where most of the grapes are grown for distilling into the head-banging brandies of Jerez. Valdepeñas reds are made from a grape they call the Cencibel – which turns out to be a very close relation of the Tempranillo grape that is the mainstay of the fine but expensive red wines of Rioja. Again, like Rioja, Valdepeñas wines are matured in oak casks to give them a vanilla-rich smoothness. Among bargain reds, Valdepeñas is a name to look out for.

Valpolicella – Red wine of Verona, Italy. Good examples have ripe, cherry fruit and a pleasingly dry finish. Unfortunately, there are many bad examples of Valpolicella. Shop with circumspection. Valpolicella Classico wines, from the best vineyards clustered around the town, are more reliable.

Those additionally labelled *superiore* have higher alcohol and some bottle age.

vanilla – Ageing wines in oak barrels (or, less picturesquely, adding oak chips to wine in huge concrete vats) imparts a range of characteristics including a smell of vanilla from the ethyl vanilline naturally given off by oak.

varietal – A varietal wine is one named after the grape variety (one or more) from which it is made. Nearly all everyday wines worldwide are now labelled in this way. It is salutary to contemplate that until the present wine boom began in the 1980s, wines described thus were virtually unknown outside Germany and one or two quirky regions of France and Italy.

vegan-friendly – My informal way of noting that a wine is claimed to have been made not only with animal-product-free finings (*see* vegetarian wine) but without any animal-related products whatsoever, such as livestock manure in the vineyards.

vegetal – A tasting note definitely open to interpretation. It suggests a smell or flavour reminiscent less of fruit (apple, pineapple, strawberry and the like) than of something leafy or even root based. Some wines are evocative (to some tastes) of beetroot, cabbage or even unlikelier vegetable flavours – and these characteristics may add materially to the attraction of the wine.

vegetarian wine – Wines labelled 'suitable for vegetarians' have been made without the assistance of animal products for 'fining' – clarifying – before bottling. Gelatine, egg whites, isinglass from fish bladders and casein from milk are among the items shunned, usually in favour of bentonite, an absorbent clay first found at Benton in the US state of Montana.

Verdejo – White grape of the Rueda region in north-west Spain. It can make superbly perfumed crisp dry whites of truly distinctive character and has helped make Rueda one of the best white-wine sources of Europe. No relation to Verdelho.

Verdelho – Portuguese grape variety once mainly used for a medium-dry style of Madeira, also called Verdelho, but now rare. The vine is now prospering in Australia, where it can make well-balanced dry whites with fleeting richness and lemon-lime acidity.

Verdicchio – White grape variety of Italy best known in the DOC zone of Castelli di Jesi in the Adriatic wine region of the Marches. Dry white wines once known for little more than their naff amphora-style bottles but now gaining a reputation for interesting, herbaceous flavours of recognisable character.

Vermentino – White grape variety principally of Italy, especially Sardinia. Makes florally scented soft dry whites.

Vieilles vignes – Old vines. Many French producers like to claim on their labels that the wine within is from vines of notable antiquity. While it's true that vines don't produce useful grapes for the first few years after planting, it is uncertain whether vines of much greater age – say 25 years plus – than others actually make better fruit. There are no regulations governing the use of the term, so it's not a reliable indicator anyway.

Vin de France – In effect, the new Vin de Table of France's morphing wine laws. The label may state the vintage (if all the wine in the blend does come from a single year's harvest) and the grape varieties that constitute the wine. It may not state the region of France from which the wine originates.

vin de liqueur – Sweet style of white wine mostly from the Pyrenean region of south-westernmost France, made by adding a little spirit to the new wine before it has fermented out, halting the fermentation and retaining sugar.

vin de pays – 'Country wine' of France. Introduced in 1968 and regularly revised ever since, it's the wine-quality designation between basic Vin de France and AOC/AOP. Although being superseded by the more recently introduced IGP (*qv*), there are more than 150 producing areas permitted to use the description vin de pays. Some vin de pays areas are huge: the Vin de Pays d'Oc (referencing the Languedoc region) covers much of the Midi and Provence. Plenty of wines bearing this humble designation are of astoundingly high quality and certainly compete with New World counterparts for interest and value. *See* Indication Géographique Protégée.

vin de table – Formerly official designation of generic French wine, now used only informally. *See* Vin de France.

vin doux naturel – Sweet, mildly fortified wine of southern France. A little spirit is added during the winemaking process, halting the fermentation by killing the yeast before it has consumed all the sugars – hence the pronounced sweetness of the wine.

vin gris – Rosé wine from Provence.

Vinho de mesa – 'Table wine' of Portugal.

Vino da tavola – The humblest official classification of Italian wine. Much ordinary plonk bears this designation, but the bizarre quirks of Italy's wine laws dictate that some of that country's finest wines are also classed as mere vino da tavola (table wine). If an expensive Italian wine is labelled as such, it doesn't mean it will be a disappointment.

Vino de la Tierra – Generic classification for regional wines, Spain. Abbreviates to VdT.

Vino de mesa – 'Table wine' of Spain. Usually very ordinary.

vintage – The grape harvest. The year displayed on bottle labels is the year of the harvest. Wines bearing no date have been blended from the harvests of two or more years.

Viognier – A white grape variety once exclusive to the northern Rhône Valley in France where it makes expensive Condrieu. Now, Viognier is grown more widely, in North and South America as well as elsewhere in France, and occasionally produces soft, marrowy whites that echo the grand style of Condrieu itself. The Viognier is now commonly blended with

Shiraz in red winemaking in Australia and South Africa. It does not dilute the colour and is confidently believed by highly experienced winemakers to enhance the quality. Steve Webber, in charge of winemaking at the revered De Bortoli estates in the Yarra Valley region of Victoria, Australia, puts between two and five per cent Viognier in with some of his Shiraz wines. 'I think it's the perfume,' he told me. 'It gives some femininity to the wine.'

Viura – White grape variety of Rioja, Spain. Also widely grown elsewhere in Spain under the name Macabeo. Wines have a blossomy aroma and are dry, but sometimes soft at the expense of acidity.

Vouvray – AC of the Loire Valley, France, known for still and sparkling dry white wines and sweet, still whites from late-harvested grapes. The wines, all from Chenin Blanc grapes, have a unique capacity for unctuous softness combined with lively freshness – an effect best portrayed in the demi-sec (slightly sweet) wines, which can be delicious and keenly priced.

Vranac – Black grape variety of the Balkans known for dense colour and tangy-bitter edge to the flavour. Best enjoyed in situ.

W

weight – In an ideal world the weight of a wine is determined by the ripeness of the grapes from which it has been made. In some cases the weight is determined merely by the quantity of sugar added during the production process. A good, genuine wine described as having weight is one in which there is plenty of alcohol and 'extract' – colour and flavour from the grapes. Wine enthusiasts judge weight by swirling the wine in the glass and then examining the 'legs' or 'tears' left clinging to the inside of the glass after the contents have subsided. Alcohol gives these runlets a dense, glycerine-like condition, and if they cling for a long time, the wine is deemed to have weight – a very good thing in all honestly made wines.

Winzergenossenschaft – One of the many very lengthy and peculiar words regularly found on labels of German wines. This means a winemaking co-operative. Many excellent German wines are made by these associations of growers.

woody – A subjective tasting note. A faintly rank odour or flavour suggesting the wine has spent too long in cask.

X

Xarel-lo – One of the main grape varieties for cava, the sparkling wine of Spain.

Xinomavro – Black grape variety of Greece. It retains its acidity even in the very hot conditions that prevail in many Greek vineyards, where harvests tend to over-ripen and make cooked-tasting wines. Modern winemaking techniques are capable of making well-balanced wines from Xinomavro.

Y

Yecla – Town and DO wine region of eastern Spain, close to Alicante, making interesting, strong-flavoured red and white wines, often at bargain prices.

yellow – White wines are not white at all, but various shades of yellow – or, more poetically, gold. Some white wines with opulent richness even have a flavour I cannot resist calling yellow – reminiscent of butter.

Z

Zibibbo – Sicilian white grape variety synonymous with north African variety Muscat of Alexandria. Scantily employed in sweet winemaking, and occasionally for drier styles.

Zierfandler – Esoteric white grape of Thermenregion, Austria. Aromatic dry wines and rare late-harvest sweet wines.

Zinfandel – Black grape variety of California. Makes brambly reds, some of which can age very gracefully, and 'blush' whites – actually pink, because a little of the skin colour is allowed to leach into the must. The vine is also planted in Australia and South America. The Primitivo of southern Italy is said to be a related variety, but makes a very different kind of wine.

Zweigelt – Black grape of Austria making juicy red wines for drinking young. Some wines are aged in oak to make interesting, heftier long-keepers.

Index